"The Great George"

CRUIKSHANK & LONDON'S GRAPHIC HUMORISTS (1800–1850)

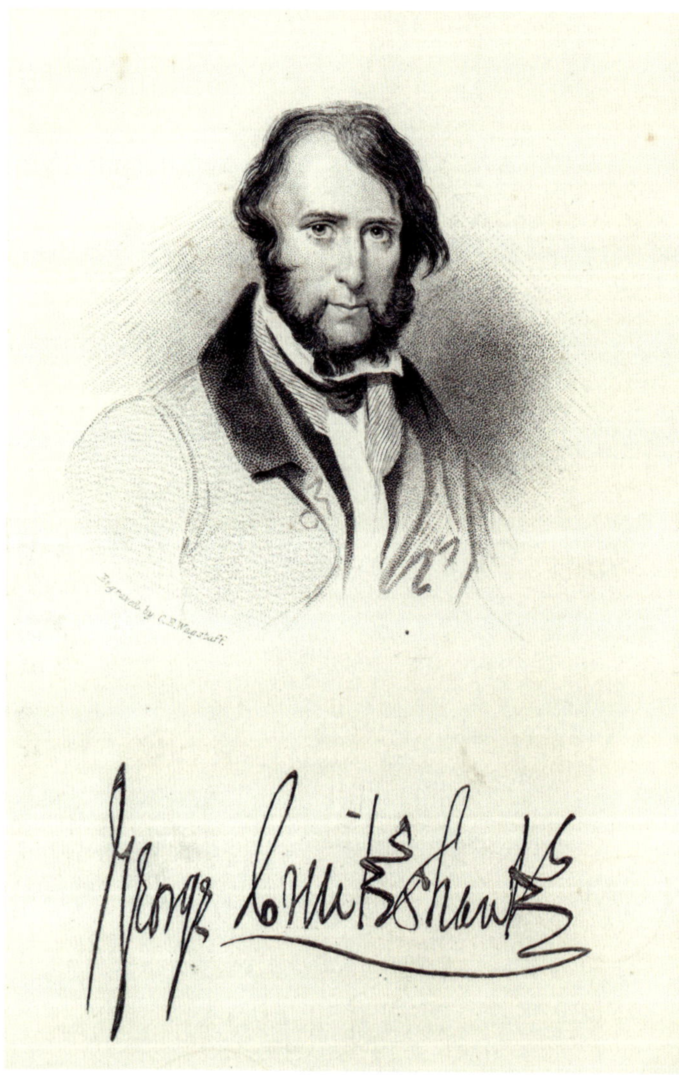

ITEM NO. 4C

"The Great George"

CRUIKSHANK & LONDON'S GRAPHIC HUMORISTS
(1800–1850)

Josephine Lea Iselin

New York
THE GROLIER CLUB
2021

This catalogue is published in connection with a Member's Exhibition at The Grolier Club

SEPTEMBER 15 – NOVEMBER 13, 2021

Cover image: Item No. 58B.

ISBN: 978-1-60583-095-7

CONTENTS

I

Introduction

THIS IS MY SECOND Grolier Club Member's Exhibition and is somewhat related to my first. I collect 19th- and 20th-century caricature, focusing on London and Paris in the first half of the 19th century. My previous exhibition, *Vive les Satiristes!: French Caricature during the Reign of Louis Philippe (1830–1848)*, told the story of Charles Philipon, the publisher who launched the great French satirical journals of the July Monarchy and, in the process, the careers of the greatest French comic artists of the time, including Honoré Daumier, J.-J. Grandville, Cham, and young Gustave Doré. The protagonist of this exhibition is George Cruikshank (1792–1878), the greatest British graphic humorist of the first three decades of the 19th century, whose working life spanned over 70 years and the reigns of the four British monarchs who ruled during the 19th century.

For a collector, political and social satire serves as a delightful window onto contemporary life of the past. In the 19th century, both English and French caricature were addressing essentially the same phenomena: a gradual transfer from monarchy to some form of representative government, the rise of the middle class, increased literacy, industrialization, and the shift from an essentially agrarian to an urban society. English caricature blossomed earlier than the French, beginning with the protean work of William Hogarth (1697–1764), whose paintings and prints laid the groundwork for generations of British satirists. Toward the end of the 18th century, as the French were embroiled in a bloody revolution, London printmakers, subject to only gentle censorship, were producing quantities of copper etchings by a number of well-known satirists, including Henry Bunbury (1750–1811), James Gillray (1756–1815), Thomas Rowlandson (1756–1827), George Murgatroyd Woodward (1765–1809),[1] and Isaac Cruikshank (1764–1811), George's father.

Once that generation passed, however, for over two decades, the son became the dominant figure in the artistry of English humor. From roughly 1811 to 1836, George Cruikshank drew the high and the low of London's society, the high with scathing satire, the low with gentle mirth, at a time when wit through illustration was of the utmost importance. Whether by his colorful copper etchings of little Boney and the Prince Regent displayed in London's print dealers' windows, or later through the books and pamphlets published primarily for his witty and endearing etchings and wood engravings, "the Great George" was a rock star, hailed by critics and sought after by publishers.

However, by the early 1840s, with the success of Mr. Dickens and the arrival of *Punch*, Cruikshank was eclipsed by a new generation of writers and artists. His quirky, distinctive drawings of boisterous Georgian London street scenes became superannuated. The author, not the illustrator, became the star. By the end of the 1840s, in constant financial need, with

1. Because of his odd middle name, Woodward was often referred to as George Moutard (Mustard) Woodward.

a sick wife who died in 1849, Cruikshank became a teetotaler; and while he continued to produce large quantities of skilled plates for novels, periodicals, and many other publications until the end of his life, he turned his prodigious talents to serve primarily the temperance movement both as an artist and as an increasingly strident preacher of abstinence. In 1850, he remarried a wife who brought him some financial and domestic stability, but – as with his first wife – no children. The fun-loving frequenter of London's pubs, the center of Georgian literary and artistic sociability, joined the ranks of the Victorian bourgeoisie, longing for recognition of his genius and acceptance as a major artist in the literary and artistic circles of London. For many of the new generation, however, he was considered an idiosyncratic genius of the past, viewed with amused disdain by those who did not wish to be lectured on the poison of alcohol.

Preparing a cogent account of George Cruikshank's life and work in such a small space is like trying to put together a large jigsaw puzzle with only a few pieces. Cruikshank worked as a professional engraver from age 14 until his death at 85. Relying solely on his pencil and etching skills for his and his family's livelihood, he was a prodigious worker, producing thousands of works on copper, steel, and wood that produced hundreds of thousands of prints over his lifetime. Collecting works by Cruikshank is like collecting beach stones; there is no way to be comprehensive. A study of Cruikshank's career is further complicated by his role as an illustrator much of whose work was done at the behest of publisher or author in the service of their ideas and projects, rather than his own. Moreover, unlike many of his contemporaries, during his long career, he not only designed the picture, but was one of the most skilled at etching it on copper, steel, or glass. Thus, the immense body of his work is highly varied and fractured, a situation that he himself chafed at more as he grew older. In 1840, as his reputation was diminishing, Cruikshank's young friend, William Makepeace Thackeray (1811–1863), aptly described how easy it was to dismiss the wonder of the artist's genius because of the disjointed nature of his work:

> [N]one of us will remember all the benefits we owe him; they have come one by one, one driving out the memory of the other: it is only when we come to examine them altogether . . . that we feel what we owe him. Look at one of Mr. Cruikshank's works, and we pronounce him an excellent humorist. Look at all, his reputation is increased by a kind of geometrical progression; as a whole diamond is a hundred times more valuable than the hundred splinters into which it might be broken would be. A fine rough English diamond is this about which we have been writing.[2]

As a person, Cruikshank was an odd fellow, full of contradictions. A passionate, theatrical man, during his youth he did much play-acting with his brother, Robert, and friend, Edmund Kean. He adored the military for its camaraderie, patriotism, and uniforms, but did not hesitate to satirize its upper ranks. From the start, he had a great moral sense of how he wished to use his etching skills, but little business sense, so he was forever looking to earn enough to keep himself and his family alive. A highly sociable loner, he was vain about his appearance. A

---

2. William Makepeace Thackeray, "An Essay on the Genius of George Cruikshank," *The Westminster Review* 34, no. 1 [1840], 59.

generous fellow, he was often in debt. A skilled engraver schooled in collaboration, he spent the last half of his life wishing to be a fine artist. Blanchard Jerrold, Cruikshank's friend and early biographer, after quoting a long disquisition by the artist on his claim to having expertise as a "cavalry man," summarized the quirkiness of Cruikshank's oversized character thusly:

> The humourist peeps through the military reformer and the military boaster, as he peeped always through Cruikshank's many grotesque masqueradings. Even his earnestness took grotesque forms. He was extravagant in all his expressions, a caricaturist even when he was most impressive. . . . He had the simplicity, also the faith, of Don Quixote.[3]

Someone recently asked me why I collect Cruikshank. Good question. First, collecting is a highly serendipitous pastime. I do not recall when and why I bought my first Cruikshank-illustrated book, but it was pure serendipity. I used to love to draw, and believe that the ability to draw humor takes great draftsmanship and a highly perceptive sense of humanity. *City of Laughter: Sex and Satire in Eighteenth-Century London,* by historian Vic Gatrell, is a study of London from 1780 to 1830 and of the importance of satire and laughter to the period. Of particular interest to me is the author's differentiation between the Hobbesian self-interest theory of the human spirit that leads in satire to snide humor, taking advantage of another's weaknesses, on the one hand, and the theories of Shaftesbury, Addison, and Steele, on the other, all of whom advocated for politeness and an ethical concern for their fellow man (woman) in writing satire.[4] Like most of the greats (think Pope, Cervantes, Balzac, Daumier, and any number of children's books), Cruikshank was never snide or nasty. Even his fiercest caricature is aesthetically pleasing and contains a kernel of the universality of the human species, as well as of the subject's individuality.

Dorothy George introduces her seminal work, *Hogarth to Cruikshank: Social Change in Graphic Satire*, as "a study of graphic social satire before the days of *Punch* and illustrated journalism when prints were engraved and sold separately."[5] George divides the period covered into three eras, that of Hogarth, George III, and the Regency.[6] Of the first two eras, she writes,

> [The 18th century] was the golden age of the English engraver. Despite the many "straight" prints – topographical, naval, military, sporting – and the more important engraving after paintings, the caricature shops had a popularity of their own. Their prints were virtually the only pictorial rendering of the flow of events, moods and fashions.[7]

---

3. Blanchard Jerrold, *The Life of George Cruikshank in Two Epochs* (London: Chatto and Windus, 1882), 1:48, 49.
4. Vic Gatrell, *City of Laughter: Sex and Satire in Eighteenth-Century London* (New York: Walker & Company, 2006), 16.
5. M. Dorothy George, *Hogarth to Cruikshank: Social Change in Graphic Satire* (New York: Walker & Company, 1967), 13.
6. The Regency was created on February 5, 1811, by the Regency Bill by which Parliament gave the Prince of Wales, George Augustus Frederick, George III's oldest son, certain limited powers of the king. It terminated on the death of George III in January 1820, when the Regent became George IV. Dorothy George defines the Regency period as follows: "[B]y common consent, 'Regency' stands for a longer period than its actual nine years – to 1830 or to 1837. Here it is taken as ending in the early thirties, with the Reform Bill and before the railway age." Ibid., 17. Gatrell's study, although titled *Eighteenth-Century,* extends to 1830.
7. George, *Hogarth to Cruikshank*, 13.

While the targets of satire may have changed from one era to another, as George's study explores, the place of the engraver and the primacy of pictorial wit endured from the 18th century through the Regency. Our George, brought up and trained as one of the last great engravers under the tutelage of the heroes of the George III era, became the preeminent artist of humor during the Regency era. He was a key transitional figure in the changing world of 19th-century London's humorous publications, carrying his graphic 18th-century-trained wit from the field of political satire during the Regency into the pre-Victorian world of journals and books, creating a whole new genre of British graphic humor, the little sketch depicting everyday life with its joys and miseries, all to be enjoyed with a smile. And in doing so for two decades, Cruikshank became a man of the people, owned by all and known as "the Great George."

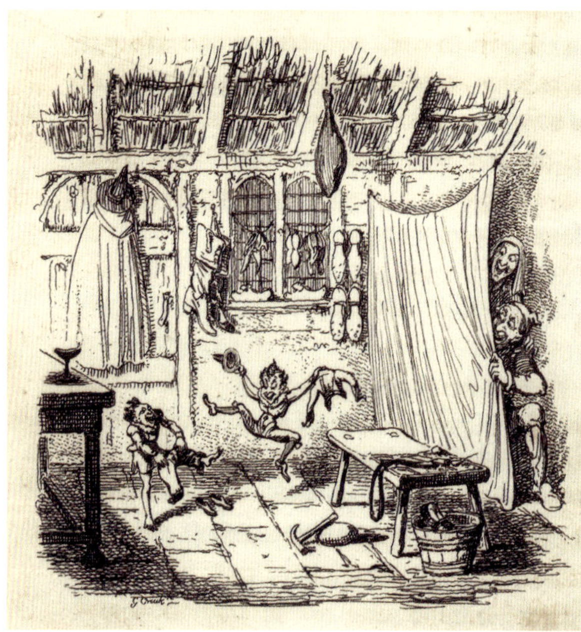

ITEM NO. 38A

II

A Brief Outline of a Long Life (1792–1878)

1792–1811: BEGINNINGS: GEORGE'S EDUCATION IN THE ART OF HUMOR

CRUIKSHANK was born in 1792 to Isaac and Mary Cruikshank three years to the day after his brother, Isaac Robert.[8] He had two younger sisters, Mary, who died in infancy, and Margaret Eliza. For most of George's youth, the family lived in a four-story house at 117 Dorset Street, in the heart of London, where Isaac's studio occupied the top floor. George and Robert had a nurse who loved to tell them fairy tales, and their mother, in addition to coloring Isaac's prints, took in lodgers to defray expenses. The boys had little formal education, but at a young age both were trained by their father in all aspects of copper etching and coloring. It was thus that they became familiar with the world of London printmaking, its artists, writers, publishers, and printshops.

In 1803, when Napoleon declared war on Great Britain, Isaac joined one of the volunteer units organized throughout London. The two brothers, emulating their father, formed units with their young buddies and, when they became eligible, signed on to volunteer units as well. In 1804, as the war heated up, Robert was commissioned as a midshipman in the East India Company. As the result of bizarre circumstances, he was left stranded on the island of St. Helena on the return trip from his maiden voyage, and reported presumed drowned. After much adventure, he reappeared in healthy form in 1806. However, by then, the relationship between the two brothers had changed. George had made great strides as an artist and had become familiar with a number of the leading humorists and their publishers. He was now receiving regular commissions for his own designs and collaborating with their father on a regular basis, thereby attaining a measure of independence and recognition in the print business unusual for a 14-year-old.[9]

ITEM NO. 93A

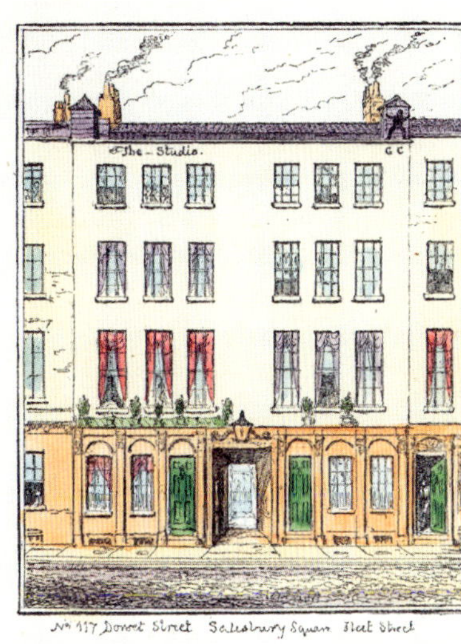

OUTSIDE THE HOUSE IN DORSET SQUARE.

---

8. Isaac Robert Cruikshank (1789–1856), generally referred to as Robert Cruikshank, signed most of his prints "I. R. Cruikshank."

9. By 1806, George had etched a number of published children's prints and lottery plates, and in January of that year, with his father's assistance, produced for John Fairburn the large folding frontispiece for *Fairburn's Edition of the Funeral* [of Admiral Horatio Nelson]. Robert L. Patten, *George Cruikshank's Life, Times and Art*

Collaboration was the norm among the small group of well-known caricaturists, many of whom were skilled engravers and regularly drew or etched for each other, as well as for other artists. For example, Isaac and Thomas Rowlandson, two of the most acclaimed engravers, etched many drawings executed by the likes of George Woodward, Henry Bunbury, and each other. As he grew in skill, George was often called upon to etch drawings by his elders. Robert Patten in his exhaustive biography of Cruikshank gives a good description of the young artist's education and the important aspects of London's printmaking trade at that time:

> George got much more from Isaac, Rowlandson, and Gillray than just etching techniques. He picked up the language of caricature – its habits of mind, characteristic subjects and treatments, imagery, and conventions. He learned who were generous publishers, who were stingy, who wanted fine-quality plates well colored, and who preferred a quick job with little background detail. He heard that Fores advertised the largest number of Napoleonic prints, that Tegg made a specialty of the Peninsular Campaign. He watched as Gillray turned out masterful images for Hannah Humphrey: erudite, complex, informed, classic in conception and execution. He observed Rowlandson's calligraphic line tracing the contours of the beautiful women and potato-faced roués, of pedants and peasants.[10]

1811–1820: YOUNG GEORGE AS POLITICAL SATIRIST

Isaac Cruikshank died in April 1811 as the result of a fatal drinking match. George Woodward had died in 1809, Henry Bunbury in 1811. By then, Gillray had become mentally unfit to produce material, and Rowlandson had retreated to social satire. While there were several other young satirists coming along in 1811, including brother Robert, George (at age 19) became the dominant political satirist in Britain and remained so for the next ten years. An interesting period, it embraced the final years and defeat of Napoleon abroad and the Regency at home, both rich targets for young George.

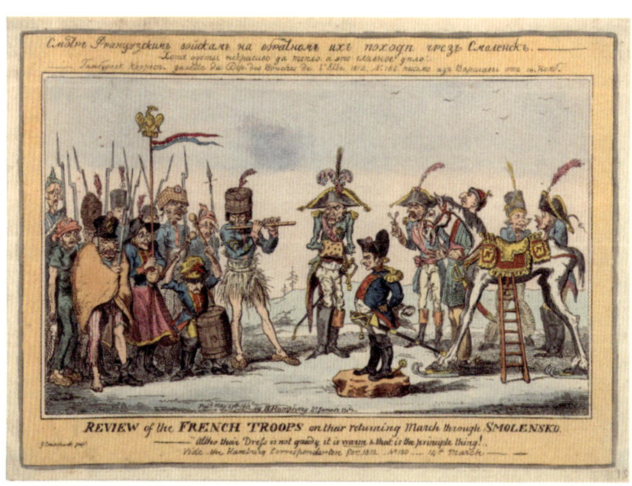

ITEM NO. 18

(New Brunswick, NJ: Rutgers University Press, 1992), 1:44, 45. See also Albert M. Cohn, *George Cruikshank, A Catalogue Raisonné of the Work Executed During the Years 1806–1877, With Collations, Notes, Approximate Values, Facsimiles, and Illustrations* (London: The Bookman's Journal, 1924), No. 284; and Cohn, Nos. 280 and 289, for Cruikshank's comic plates published by Fairburn in 1806 and 1807.

10. Patten, *George Cruikshank's Life*, 1:87.

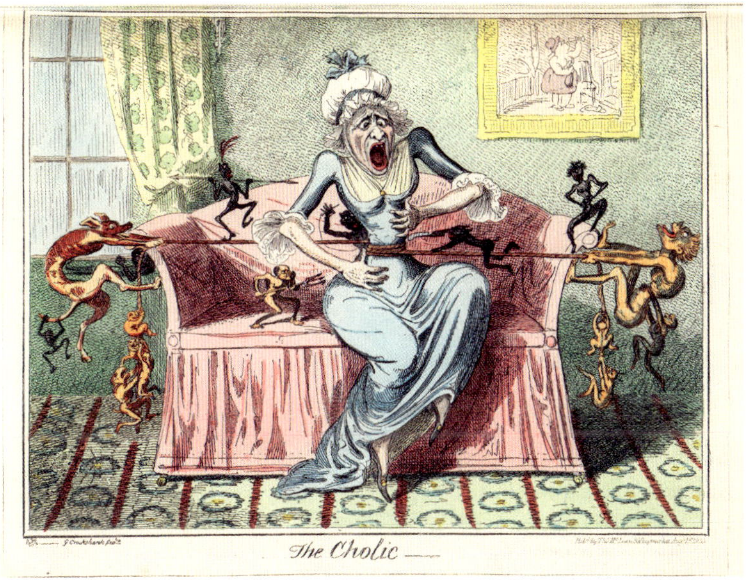

ITEM NO. 4B

Cruikshank's success lay not only in the quality and humor of his work, the skill and speed with which he could turn out the design and etch the copper, but also in the virulence of his attacks on two of the nation's most unpopular figures, "Boney" and the profligate Prince of Wales. In mid-1811, he became the principal contributor of plates for *The Scourge*, a new monthly journal devoted to caricature, published by James Johnson from 1811 through 1816.[11] He provided prints on a regular basis to many other dealers as well, including the high priestess, Hannah Humphrey,[12] her nephew, George Humphrey, Thomas Tegg, and W. N. Jones. George also developed close relationships with William Combe, creator of the famous *Dr. Syntax* series,[13] and with William Hone, the radical publisher,[14] both of which were of key importance to his rising recognition as a leading political caricaturist. In 1815, he provided Combe with 30 engraved plates for *The Life of Napoleon, a Hudibrastic Poem in Fifteen Cantos, by Doctor Syntax;* and from 1819–1821, he collaborated with Hone on a series of over 40 political tracts making fun of the Regent, his errant wife, Queen Caroline, and the political system then in place. These tracts, prolifically illustrated with wood engravings designed by Cruikshank, were enormously popular and went to many editions within a year of first publication. While young George was often labeled a radical as a result of his work for *The Scourge* and Hone, his etching talents served a whole range of publishers from a whole range of political and social views during this early period.

---

11. Cruikshank prepared 41 of the 72 foldout, hand-colored etchings that were the lead entries to each month's edition of the *Scourge.* Significantly, only his etchings were signed.
12. Hannah Humphrey died in 1818, leaving her print shop in St. James Place to her nephew, George Humphrey.
13. In 1812, Rudolph Ackermann published *The Tour of Dr. Syntax in Search of the Pittoresque*, Combe's satire on 18th-century romanticized travelogues of the English countryside, essentially a vehicle for Rowlandson's amusing aquatints. The volumes and editions that followed were wildly successful and engendered a number of sequels.
14. In 1816 and 1817, Hone published a number of pamphlets parodying the Church of England for which he was criminally prosecuted three separate times. George worked with Hone on his defense before the Chief Justice, Lord Ellenborough, and helped secure his acquittal on all charges.

1821–1835: WHEN HUMOROUS ETCHING WAS KING

As the third decade of the century began, illustrated books and journals gained currency over single prints, particularly where humor was involved. Illustrations were popular for serialized books, published in parts or magazines that were then published in book form, as well as for books themselves, often filled with a new genre: a collection of illustrated humorous urban sketches that were in great demand as literacy increased and the urban population grew. Two new techniques of printing illustrations, wood engraving and lithography, encouraged this trend.[15]

The period 1820 to 1823 was a major turning point in Cruikshank's career. While occasionally he continued to provide George Humphrey, John Fairburn, and other publishers with single plates for political satire, he essentially turned to humorous illustration and social satire in the expanding world of journals and illustrated books.[16] In 1821, George and Robert made their first foray into book illustration, collaborating with Pierce Egan as author, to produce *Life in London.* Egan was known as "the first gentleman" of the London sporting scene of wrestling, boxing, and bull-baiting. Each of the three collaborators claimed to have originated the idea of an urban travelogue describing the peccadilloes of three comrades in different venues in London. The work, with its 36 humorous hand-colored etchings and numerous wood-engraved vignettes, which first came out in 12 monthly parts, was enormously popular, succeeded by a number of editions and sequels, in effect following up on the great success of Combe's *Dr. Syntax* series.[17]

---

15. In the 1770s, the engraver, Thomas Bewick (1753–1828), adapted metal-engraving tools to cut hard boxwood across the grain, producing printing blocks that could be used with metal type and were much more durable than traditional woodcuts, allowing high-quality illustration of written material at a low price. By the mid-1820s, Bewick had trained several generations of wood engravers, and the technique was at its high point.

Lithography, invented in 1798 by a German, Alois Senefelder, was brought to France and Britain early in the 19th century. In France, by 1830, Charles Philipon was creating his famous publishing empire of satire based primarily on lithographic prints. Ironically, in Britain, because of its ease in creating images in large numbers with great skill and satisfactory impressions, lithography was considered "cheap and unworthy to artists accustomed to the small editions obtained from copper plates." Gordon N. Ray, *The Illustrator and the Book in England from 1790 to 1914* (New York: The Pierpont Morgan Library, Oxford University Press, 1976), 51. However, by the mid-1820s, lithographs were used in several new magazines devoted primarily to political satire, such as William Heath's *Glasgow Looking Glass*, and Thomas McLean's *Looking Glass*. The principal satiric artists in these journals were Robert Seymour, Charles Jameson Grant, and John Doyle ("HB").

For studies of political satire during the period 1825–1841, see Ian Haywood, *The Rise of Victorian Caricature* (Cham, Switzerland: Palgrave Macmillan, an imprint of Springer Nature Switzerland AG [2020]); Brian Maidment, "Graphic Satire, Caricature, Comic Illustration and the Radical Press, 1820–1845," in *Journalism and the Periodical Press in Nineteenth-Century Britain*, ed. Joanne Shattuck, 84–103 (Cambridge: Cambridge University Press, 2017), doi:10.1017/9781316084403.007.

16. Cruikshank's reduced participation in political satire may be attributed in part to the fact that, in June 1820, George IV (who as Regent had long fought Cruikshank's attacks by ordering the purchase of many of his more objectionable plates), paid Cruikshank one hundred pounds "in consideration of a pledge not to caricature His Majesty in any immoral situation . . ." Patten, *George Cruikshank's Life,* 1:176, 177.

17. See, e.g., *Life in Paris* by David Carey, published in 1822 by John Fairburn, illustrated by George Cruikshank; *Pearce Egan's Finish to the Adventures of Tom, Jerry, and Logic, in their pursuits through Life in and out of London:* Illustrated by the pencil of Mr. Robert Cruikshank, in 36 Scenes from Real Life, & enriched with several Designs on Wood by the same Artist. Printed by C. Bayne. 1830.

Life in London, with its full-page illustrations of young dandies carousing around the city, clearly reflected the tastes of late Georgian London, as well as the boisterous life of drinking and sporting that George and Robert had led during their twenties while living in Dorset Street with their mother and sister. But this was to change. In 1818, Robert married and shortly had a son, Percy. In 1823, Robert and George's mother, Mary, leased a house in Pentonville, a suburb of London, in an effort to reduce costs, and George moved in with her. The following year, George married Mary Ann Walker, a distant cousin whom he had known for some time. He leased a house near his mother's and the next year moved to Amwell Street, also in Pentonville, where he and Mary Ann lived until her death in 1849. Just short of her 17th birthday when she married, Mary Ann appears to have been mature for her age, but her health was fragile. So while it seems to have been a happy marriage, Mary Ann was frequently ill, and they had no children. Thus, by age 32, our artist had moved to the suburbs, far from the publishing hub of London and the bustle of the Strand, and was responsible for the support of a wife and his own household.

In 1823, the publisher Charles Baldwyn asked Cruikshank to illustrate the books that were to launch his career as a book illustrator. In the short period before Baldwyn died in 1824, publisher and artist produced *Points of Humour, Parts I and II* (1823, 1824), *German Popular Stories* (1823), and *Mornings at Bow Street* (1824), each illustrating short, humorous tales with tiny, amusing, but beautifully executed etchings or wood engravings. As Baldwyn stated in the preface to *Points of Humour, Part I*, p. iii, a group of short sketches collected by Henry Southern,

> . . . the literary part of this work is of humble pretensions. One object alone has been aimed . . . to select or to invent those incidents which [would] afford scope to the peculiar talents of the artist who adorns them with his designs.

Points of Humour was a tremendous success, engendering an important article by the critic John Gibson Lockhart (1794–1854), a Scottish writer and editor best known as the author of a much-lauded biography of his father-in-law, Sir Walter Scott. In the article, "On George Cruikshank," Lockhart praised him as "a thorough-bred artist," and urged him to rival Hogarth as a fine artist.[18] Baldwyn, in his Preface to *Points of Humour, Part II*, p. v, responded to Lockhart:

> It has been said that it is a pity that Mr. Cruikshank should waste his talents upon ephemeral anecdotes, and not hand down his name by illustrating the works of our great Novelists [Fielding and Smollett]. As well it might have been said to these great Novelists "confine yourselves to commenting upon or translating Cervantes or Le Sage.". . . Hogarth did not paint his *Rakes Progress* in illustration of any immortal work. . .to remind posterity of his existence. A similar excuse may apply to Cruikshank, who, generally, would chuse [*sic*] rather to exalt the humble, than endow the rich.

Lockhart's praise and admonition to use his talents toward higher artistic ends stayed with Cruikshank for the rest of his life.

Baldwyn, a great friend and supporter of young George, died in October 1824 just as *Points*

---

18. Patten, *George Cruikshank's Life,* 1:242, 243.

of Humour Part II went to press. At his death, most of his publishing projects, including his partnership with Cruikshank, passed to James Robins, the next influential publisher in Cruikshank's life. In the course of their work together, Cruikshank came to know Baldwyn's 14-year-old niece, Eliza, who became his second wife in 1850.

By the end of the 1820s, Cruikshank's reputation had grown to the point that he was able to arrange for a writer to "write up" his sketches, and designed and etched a number of albums containing his own comic drawings, full of verbal and visual puns, which he either published himself or arranged to be published through Robins.[19] In most instances where the writer's name was even disclosed on the title page, it has long since been forgotten, while George's name, always emblazoned there as the principal selling point, is recognizable by many even today.[20] In a highly delightful, detailed, and laudatory review of the album *Phrenological Illustrations,* published in *Blackwood's Edinburgh Magazine* in 1826, Christopher North, the influential scholar and art critic, summarized Cruikshank's genius, saying (through his alter ego, "Tickler"), "[Cruikshank is] far more than the Prince of Caricaturists . . . he has a clear insight through the exterior of manners into the passions of the heart."[21] In sum, by 1826, the power of his popularity allowed Cruikshank the freedom to draw whatever was his fancy, and he did some of his best and wittiest work. The public loved him, and he became known as "the Great George." Illustration was king.

It is worth pausing here to learn something of Cruikshank's method of working. Martin Hardie, in his *English Colored Books,* describes Cruikshank's routine as follows:

> Cruikshank's published work conveys no idea of the painstaking study and the endless elaboration by which it was produced. For every illustration he would make several sketches in pencil or ink, and it was his habit to add in the margin, as he worked, numerous little studies of figures, suggesting an alteration in position or in features, often expressed in a few lines, yet always full of animation. Whether his illustration was intended to be published in colours or not, he often finished his pencil drawing in water-colour, perhaps because he obtained by this means a better feeling of light, shade, and atmosphere, and could enter better into the spirit of the scene. His colouring, it should be said, was of the simplest, consisting of slight washes of yellow, green and blue, in pure tints, with here and there a suggestion of red. From the drawing thus completed he made a pencil tracing to be transferred to the copper for etching. If the illustration were to be published in a coloured state, a proof of the etching was tinted by the artist. With this as a model, hundreds of similarly tinted copies were produced by the colourists working for the publisher. . . .[22]

---

19. See, e.g., *Phrenological Illustrations, Or an Artist's View of the Craniological System of Doctors Gall and Spurzheim* (1826); *Illustrations of Time* (1827); *Scraps and Sketches, Parts 1 and 2* (1828, 1829); *My Sketch Book* (1834–1836), Item Nos. 43A, 43B, and 43D.

20. As an indication of Cruikshank's preeminence as humorous artist at this time, the work of his most skilled contemporary, Robert Seymour (1798–1836), who began work as an illustrator in the early 1820s and became one of the best-known humorous artists in London for the brief period before his early death in 1836, went unsigned until he became the principal artist for *Figaro in London* in 1832. See Brian Maidment, "The Draughtsman's Contacts: Robert Seymour and the Humorous Periodical Press in the 1830s," *Journal of European Periodical Studies* 1, no. 1 (Summer 2016): 38–40.

21. Quoted in Patten, *George Cruikshank's Life,* 1:287, 288.

22. Martin Hardie, *English Colored Books* (New York: G. P. Putnam's Sons; London: Methuen and Co., 1906), 193. For some good examples of both Cruikshank's penciled sketches and "little studies of figures" in the margins, see copies of leaves from the Zukor Album, Item Nos. 53A and 53B; and for the method and style of his coloring,

Cruikshank paid a life-long price for his celebrity. His style was often copied, his works misappropriated, and the Cruikshank name used not infrequently in order to mislead. Any such incidence rankled George immensely. In defense, he made rather a thing about his signature and loved giving autographs, signing virtually all his works with his full name or "G. Cruikshank" or "GCk." Among the offenders in misleading the public in their use of the Cruikshank name were his brother Robert's publisher, William Kidd, and later Robert's son, Percy Cruikshank. In 1827, Robert Seymour started signing his witty drawings "Shortshanks" until Cruikshank objected. But the most egregious outright taking was by *Bell's Life in London,* a weekly sporting magazine started in 1822 and by 1825 owned and published by William Innell Clement. As a favor to its editor, his friend Vincent Dowling, Cruikshank had allowed two of his prints to be used in the magazine. However, this was followed by the continuing use of many more of Cruikshank's works without permission.[23] By December 1827, Robins was threatening action against Clement.[24]

In the fall of 1834, Charles Tilt and the periodical writer James Vizetelly proposed publishing an almanac as a parody of the straight-laced *Old Moore's Almanack,*[25] and asked Cruikshank to provide the illustrations. *The Comic Almanack for the Year 1835 with Twelve Illustrations of the Months, by Geo. Cruikshank,* published in December 1835, was the perfect foil for Cruikshank's talents, its main attraction being his 12 witty drawings of London by month. Scholar Brian Maidment describes the *Almanack*'s economic appeal, and how it fit into the reformist era of the mid-1830s:

> *The Comic Almanack* was undoubtedly the most sustained and successful satirical almanac that appeared in the late-Regency to early-Victorian period, but it was only part of a widespread recognition of the genre's comic possibilities that emerged in the mid-1830s. Such recognition was constructed out of a complex of print-cultural factors. The earnestness of the Society for the Diffusion of Useful Knowledge's (SDUK) critique of the predictive almanac's carnivalesque delight in the improbable and the miraculous undoubtedly alienated many. For a wide number of publishers, readers, and writers, print forms that sought authority and used information as a form of potentially coercive social management were to be treated with suspicion or disdain, especially when they originated from the Whig-sponsored program of Lord Brougham,[26]

---

see the original watercolor drawings for the illustrations for *Cinderella,* Item Nos. 85D and 85E. One of the most interesting reproductions of Cruikshank's watercolor illustrations is to be found in *Cruikshank's Water Colours, with Introduction by Joseph Grego* (London: A. & C. Black, 1903).

23. Cohn states that 26 different woodcuts signed "GCk" were published in *Bell's Life in London* at different times; that on June 22, 1828, one issue had 34 additional Cruikshank woodcuts without signature, and that the magazine used many of Cruikshank images to provide the headings for the news columns for its "The Gallery of 140 Comicalities." Cohn, *George Cruikshank, A Catalogue Raisonné,* 67; see also Patten, *George Cruikshank's Life,* 1:300, 301.

24. See original manuscript letter from Robins to Cruikshank, dated 24 December, 1827, Item No. 33C.

25. Francis Moore (1657–1715) wrote and published what later became *Old Moore's Almanack,* which first appeared in 1697 and still appeared yearly in the 1830s.

26. Lord Brougham (1778–1868) was a liberal British statesman who became Lord Chancellor in Lord Grey's Ministry, and played a prominent role in passing the 1832 Reform Act and 1833 Slavery Abolition Act. He developed strong views about education during this time. Wikipedia, s.v. "Henry Brougham, 1st Baron Brougham and Vaux," accessed June 8, 2020, https://en.wikipedia.org/wiki/Henry_Brougham,_1st_Baron_Brougham_and_Vaux.

ITEM NO. 55A

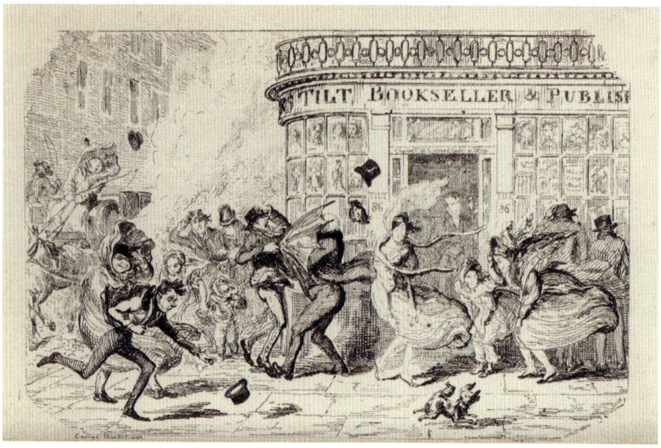

Charles Knight, and the SDUK.... Additionally, the rapid evolution of the market for print commodities between 1820 and 1840 was beginning to offer new economic possibilities and a broad readership willing to be diverted rather than informed to opportunistic publishers.... The traditional graphic construction of the almanac form, with its tables, rules, and mixture of graphic and typeset elements, was both familiar and attractive to a mass readership and thus amenable to comic reworking. All of these factors combined to make the invention of travesty and satirical almanacs if not inevitable then at least highly likely.[27]

The 1835 *Comic Almanack* was an immediate success, published annually thereafter for another 18 years under George's management, providing him with his primary, if modest, source of regular income for many years.

1835–1840: THE ARRIVAL OF MR. DICKENS

By the early 1830s, the world of publishing in England was changing again, as was the country. William IV, third son of George III, succeeded his older brother in June 1830. Georgian England became a thing of the past. The new king, a Royal Navy man and a hard worker, eschewed the extravagant lifestyle of his brother. The Industrial Revolution was picking up steam. There was great unrest in both the cities and the countryside, and reform was on the move. On William's ascension, the Tory administration of the Duke of Wellington gave way to the Whigs and the reformist prime minister Lord Grey. Amidst much clamor, Grey was able to pass the 1832 Reform Act, the first of several bills adopted by Parliament in the next decade getting rid of the rotten boroughs, increasing the franchise, and addressing extreme poverty and other serious problems caused by the new industrialized economy. William died in 1837 with many illegitimate children but no heir. His niece, Victoria, daughter of his deceased brother the Duke of Kent, came to the throne, and thus began a 64-year reign, during which Great Britain became the dominant country in the world, with great wealth from a large overseas empire and a parliamentary system of government achieved without revolution.

By 1835, as Cruikshank was launching his *Comic Almanack*, the public was becoming enamored of the 19th-century novel – long, extended stories, often first serialized monthly in parts

27. Brian Maidment, "'Larks in Season': *The Comic Almanack* (1835–54)," *Cahiers victoriens et édouardiens* [Enligne], 84 Automne | 2016, mis enligne le 01 novembre 2016, consulté le 22 avril 2017, http://cve.revues.org/2881, doi:10.4000/cve.2881. The Society for the Diffusion of Useful Knowledge was an earnest organization founded in 1826, mainly at the instigation of Lord Brougham, with the object of publishing inexpensive texts intended to adapt scientific and similarly high-minded material for the rapidly expanding, but less educated, reading public. It was wound up in 1848. Wikipedia, s.v. "Society for the Diffusion of Useful Knowledge," accessed July 18, 2020, https://en.wikipedia.org/wiki/Society_for_the_Diffusion_of_Useful_Knowledge.

or journals and then published in book form, with or without illustrations. As the market for journals, pamphlets, and books expanded further, the predominant role of the comic artist in London gave way to the dominance of the author, editor, and publisher. One of Cruikshank's biographers describes this shift as follows:

> The distinctions between journalism and literature that seem so obvious to us today were, in early Victorian London, by no means so clear-cut. Not only were novels regularly published in periodical form, but their authors were almost invariably the founder, proprietor, or editor of a magazine at some stage in their careers.[28]

As a result of this trend, the comic illustrator lost not only his primacy in the creative process, but also much of its financial rewards. In general, the artist continued to be paid per plate provided to the publisher, who retained the copyrights. The author, however, as noted above, not only created content, but often was the editor of a journal controlling the writers and illustrators to be published, and therefore was in a much better position to demand a larger share of the profits from the publisher. This shift in creative and financial power is demonstrated by the publication history of the first three books authored by young Charles Dickens (1812–1870): *Sketches by Boz*, *Pickwick Papers*, and *Oliver Twist*, all three published both serially and in volume form in only three years (1836–1838). Ironically, the neophyte author was brought to fame in record time by two seasoned and well-known illustrators – George Cruikshank, who illustrated *Boz* and *Oliver Twist*, and Robert Seymour, who initiated *Pickwick*.

Sketches by Boz

In the summer of 1835, William Harrison Ainsworth (1805–1882), one of London's best-known authors, and John Macrone, a young editor in London, asked Cruikshank to illustrate the fourth edition of Ainsworth's yet-unillustrated but highly popular novel, *Rookwood*. Macrone had also started a journal, *Monthly Magazine*, that had just published five sketches written by Dickens, then a reporter of Parliamentary proceedings for the *Morning Chronicle*. He suggested to Dickens the publication of a series of his sketches illustrated by Cruikshank. Dickens, a 23-year-old unknown at the time, jumped at the idea of having "the Great George" introduce his work to the public. Cruikshank was laden with commissions as well as his ongoing obligations to the still unfinished *1835 Almanack*. However, his work was full of risk; he was often stiffed by those to whom he delivered designs and plates, and therefore was chronically in need of funds. So by fall of 1835, once his plates for the *Almanack* were under control, he agreed to take on Dickens's yet-untitled work.

Dickens's sketches of everyday life in London and Cruikshank's depiction of its bustling life of shopkeepers, housewives, and children were a perfect match. *Sketches by Boz, Illustrative of Every-Day Life, and Every-Day People, in Two Volumes. Illustrations by George Cruikshank* was published by Macrone in early February 1836, and was a great success. The one-volume *Sketches by Boz, Second Series*, was published in late December 1836 (with an 1837 publication date). Dickens's gratitude for George's contribution to his first publishing venture was effusive:

---

28. Michael Wynn Jones, *George Cruikshank: His Life and London* (London: Macmillan London Limited, 1978), 80.

> In humble imitation of a prudent course, universally adopted by aeronauts, the Author of these volumes throws them up as his pilot balloon, trusting it may catch some favourable current, and devoutly and earnestly hoping it may *go off well*– . . . Entertaining no inconsiderable feeling of trepidation, at the idea of making so perilous a voyage in so frail a machine, alone and unaccompanied, the Author was naturally desirous to secure the assistance and companionship of some well-known individual, who had frequently contributed to the success, though his well-earned reputation rendered it impossible for him ever to have shared the hazard, of similar undertakings. To whom, as possessing this requisite in an eminent degree, could he apply but to GEORGE CRUIKSHANK? The application was readily heard and at once acceded to: this is their first voyage in company, but it may not be the last.[29]

Producing the two series of *Sketches by Boz* was not done without strain on both author and illustrator. While surely some stress is inherent in any such collaboration, especially where the work is created in monthly installments, the strain was aggravated here by the expectations of the ambitious young author, and the busy schedules of both creators. In addition to preparing his new work, Dickens was still reporting full time on the proceedings of Parliament, as well as writing and producing an operetta. Cruikshank, busy with his many other commissions and projects, often executed designs that had to be discarded because Dickens changed the story. Dickens often failed to give Cruikshank manuscript when the artist had time to design and etch; and Cruikshank often did not provide the plates as quickly as the impatient young author wished. The production of the *Sketches, Second Series,* was further stressed by the publication in March 1836 of the first of the 20 monthly parts of *The Posthumous Papers of the Pickwick Club* by Chapman and Hall, at which point Dickens became immersed in the monthly adventures of Mr. Pickwick. And in November, both author and artist agreed to participate in a new humorous monthly magazine to be published by Richard Bentley, entitled *Bentley's Miscellany*, Dickens as editor and contributor, Cruikshank as the journal's exclusive artist.

Added to the stress created by these numerous obligations was another, more subtle irritant: a different concept of their roles in the creative process. Cruikshank, honed in the Georgian era when the picture was equal to, if not more important than, the text, had always collaborated in the conception and execution of the works he was called on to illustrate. The young ambitious author, however, had other ideas. So, for example, *Sketches Second Series* almost came to naught when Dickens, annoyed by Cruikshank's frequent suggestions, had his manuscript set in type before having it delivered to Cruikshank for illustration. Cruikshank became so upset that initially he refused to provide plates, writing to Macrone,

> I did expect to see that MS from time to time in order that I might have the privilege of suggesting any little alterations to suit the Pencil, but if you are printing the book all that sort of thing is out of the question. Only this much I must say, that unless I can get good subjects to work upon, I will not work at all.

Dickens's response to the publisher was swift and cutting:

> I have long believed Cruikshank to be mad. . .I am very much amused at the notion of his altering my manuscript, and that had it fallen into his hands, I should have preserved his emendations as "curiosities of Literature."[30]

---

29. Preface to Vol. I of first edition of *Sketches by Boz,* First Series, cited above.
30. Wynn Jones, *George Cruikshank: His Life,* 65.

All was soon smoothed over; the *Second Series* was published in December 1836, and both series were wildly successful, receiving much praise from the critics. In his review of the First Series in the *Evening Standard*, George Hogarth, Dickens's father-in-law, named Cruikshank "the modern Hogarth" and opined,

> The illustrations . . . are beautiful and highly finished etchings, admirable as pieces of art, and full of the truth, nature, grotesque humour, and irresistible drollery, which distinguish this unrivalled artist. Nothing can excel the ability with which he has embodied the conceptions of his coadjutor, and placed before the very eyes of the reader, the scenes and characters which "Boz" has presented to his imagination.[31]

However, the glowing reviews, putting author and illustrator on the same plain, clearly rankled young Dickens. His paean of gratitude to Cruikshank that had appeared in the "Preface" to the First Series (quoted above) never appeared again.

The Pickwick Papers

An oft-asked question is why Cruikshank did not illustrate more of Dickens's works. Much of the answer lies in happenstance and in the timing and genesis of *The Pickwick Papers*. In the fall of 1835, the idea for *Pickwick* was brought to Chapman and Hall, a well-established publishing firm, by Seymour, whose concept was for a group of illustrated anecdotes making fun of newly rich gentlemen wanting to up their place in society by participating in such country sporting activities as hunting, fishing, and shooting. The artist had already published five volumes of highly amusing lithographs depicting expeditions of overequipped and undertrained Cockneys pursuing cats, birds, and stray pigs on foot and on horseback, in the popular series *Sketches by Seymour*. The publishers were taken with the proposal and approached Dickens to see if he would supply the letterpress. Dickens accepted, but boldly made clear that he was not a sporting person and would not write the hack text as proposed, but stories to be illustrated. He proposed terms that he hoped would allow him to leave his day job at the *Morning Chronicle*. Chapman and Hall, wanting to initiate the project quickly, and recognizing a talented young writer, agreed to Dickens's conditions. Thus, the order of the creative process was reversed: the author would tell the story, the artist would provide the illustrations – as requested.

As could be anticipated, the relationship between artist and author quickly deteriorated. In April 1836, after Seymour had illustrated the first two installments of *Pickwick*, and only days after arguing with Dickens over his latest illustration, Seymour shot himself.[32] In searching for Seymour's replacement, Dickens, aware of Cruikshank's busy schedule (including the etchings for *Sketches by Boz, Second Series)*, and needing immediate help, never approached Cruikshank. Robert Buss was hired, but after providing two drawings was found lacking. Thackeray and Hablot Knight Browne (1815–1882) applied with samples of their sketches. Dickens preferred Browne's, which bore a strong similarity to Cruikshank's.[33] The author

31. Patten, *George Cruikshank's Life*, 2:20.
32. For several years Seymour had struggled with mental illness and had had a breakdown in 1830.
33. In 1870, after Dickens's death, Cruikshank wrote to a friend, "The Public at one time supposed that I had adopted the name of 'Phiz' to illustrate the works of 'Boz,' . . . & the reason why many believed them to be by me was because my style of work was closely imitated." Patten, *George Cruikshank's Life*, 2:17.

must also have recognized how much easier it would be to deal with a younger, more adaptable illustrator just beginning his career than with the celebrated artist 20 years his senior. Thus, a long friendship and fruitful collaboration began between Boz and Phiz.

Oliver Twist

Oliver Twist was published in 24 monthly installments in the new *Bentley's Miscellany* from February 1837 through January 1939, with two Cruikshank etchings in each installment. The three-volume book was rushed to publication by Bentley in mid-November 1838, urged by Dickens so that the cliff-hanger end of Oliver's story would not appear in the *Miscellany* to spoil sales of the book. Dickens was a canny businessman. The series and the book were highly successful even though they had to compete with *Pickwick* for much of its two-year serialization. Just as with *Sketches by Boz*, there were difficulties coordinating illustrations with story under the stress of monthly deadlines, exacerbated by both men's crowded schedules. Collaboration between author and illustrator was further complicated by disputes arising between Dickens and two of his publishers, Macrone and Bentley, each of which had a substantial adverse effect on Cruikshank. Essentially, both disputes arose from the fact that by mid-1837 – with major assistance from Seymour and Cruikshank – Dickens had become a hot property, with three bestsellers on the market published by three different publishers.

ITEM NO. 62B

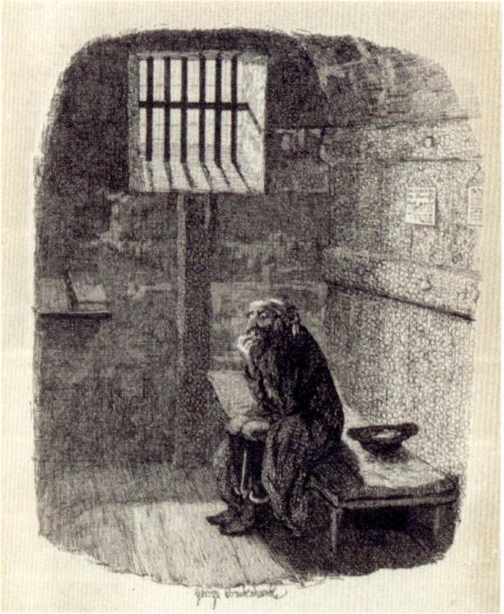

The falling out with Macrone began in June 1837 when Dickens learned that the publisher, sole owner of the copyrights and strapped for cash, intended to reissue both series of *Sketches by Boz* in monthly parts, clearly trying to profit from the immense popularity of *Pickwick* and *Oliver Twist.* Dickens was not only enraged by what he perceived as the disloyalty and unjust enrichment of the publisher, but also concerned that monthly publication of *Sketches* at that time would eat into monthly sales of his other two books. After extended negotiations, Dickens persuaded Chapman and Hall to buy the copyrights to *Sketches by Boz,* both series, from Macrone, with Cruikshank's 28 copperplates thrown into the bargain *gratis.*[34]

The falling out with Bentley resulted from much the same dynamic. By August 1837, the ambitious author, having become overextended and convinced that he was not paid enough for his work, sought to raise his editing fee and extend the time in which he was obligated to deliver to Bentley his next novel, *Barnaby Rudge,* which was to follow *Oliver Twist* in the *Miscellany.* The dispute raged on for months. Editor and publisher were not even on speaking terms. Dickens enlisted Cruikshank to mediate and to act as his go-between with Bentley regarding his editorial duties. Finally, in February 1839, Dickens resigned as editor and took *Barnaby Rudge* with him.[35] Certainly Cruikshank profited little from any of these distracting disputes.

34. Ibid., 2:61, 62.

35. *Barnaby Rudge* was published in 1841 by Dickens himself in his short-lived weekly, *Master Humphrey's Clock.*

Indeed, he lost the opportunity to illustrate Dickens's next novel and perhaps others, and was never even given a place at the table as Dickens and his two publishers divided the substantial profits generated, in no small part, by Cruikshank's illustrations for *Sketches* and *Oliver*.

The same tension between Dickens and Cruikshank concerning the extent of the artist's collaboration in the creative process arose again in connection with *Oliver Twist*, but in a different time frame. It was long built into the mythology around George Cruikshank that as he grew older, he became bitter and deluded into claiming to have been responsible for the plot and a number of the characters in *Oliver Twist*. While it is true that in his elder years, Cruikshank passionately defended his part in the creative process of his work with Dickens, as Wynn Jones takes pains to document, he never claimed to have written any of the novel, only to have proposed "the bare outline of a plot to Dickens and in some specific instances made concrete suggestions about characterization and location."[36] The historian also notes that Cruikshank made these modest claims only in 1871 (after Dickens's death) to correct the record "in the wake of a squabble between John Foster and another of Dickens's biographers," one of whom was labeling Cruikshank a malicious liar. After an extensive analysis of contemporary documents, Wynn Jones concludes that Cruikshank's claims were fully justified.[37] Patten supports this view, prefacing his detailed examination of the record with the following comment on the acrimonious exchange of articles and letters accusing the elderly Cruikshank of false claims:

> The exchange pinpointed the nub of the quarrel. Neither Forster nor most of his mid-Victorian contemporaries thought of illustrations as other than subordinate to the dictates of the writer... Dickens had been influential in establishing the dominance of author over illustrator: Browne proved tractable, as did his successors ... But Dickens did not start out his career with that measure of control.[38]

Despite the tensions attending their collaborations, Cruikshank and Dickens remained good friends and companions during and after *Oliver* – at least for the next 15 years. They continued to collaborate on a number of projects including *Memoires of Grimaldi* and *The Lonely Ballard of Lord Bateman*, and entertained each other and their spouses not infrequently. As Wynn Jones notes,

> On a personal level their friendship blossomed, the two men drawn together by their clubbable natures and passions for the theatre. George became an active member of Dickens's amateur theatrical group which performed in London in the 1840s and once went on a long tour of the provinces ... [V]ery likely it was George's artlessly theatrical manner in company that endeared him to the writer.[39]

In retrospect, Cruikshank's career as book illustrator reached its apogee with *Sketches by Boz* and *Oliver Twist*. For the first and last time, the celebrated illustrator of London's scenes

36. Wynn Jones, *George Cruikshank: His Life*, 67.
37. Ibid., 67–71.
38. Patten, *George Cruikshank's Life*, 2:481–485.
39. Wynn Jones, *George Cruikshank: His Life*, 65; see also Jerrold, *Cruikshank in Two Epochs*, 1:238, for the continued Cruikshank-Dickens friendship.

of joy and misery was collaborating with the man who became the celebrated novelist of London's scenes of joy and misery. They were both passionate reformers, working during an era of reform. And because the young author was just getting his literary feet under him, Cruikshank's ideas concerning London's orphan's houses, prisons, and under-life, captured so well in his copper etchings for *Oliver*, played an integral part in the success of both books. His engravings on steel for Ainsworth's historical novels that were to follow were of a different genre.[40] The whimsy and animation of the scenes of the Dodger and Fagin in grim hovels were replaced with beautiful renderings of famous buildings and famous people, lacking some of the earthiness and spontaneity that were Cruikshank's special gifts.

1841–1847: CRUIKSHANK'S DISPUTES WITH BENTLEY AND AINSWORTH; HIS REJECTION OF OFFERS FROM MESSRS. DICKENS AND PUNCH

In early 1839, Ainsworth replaced Dickens as editor of *Bentley's Miscellany* and over the next five years wrote six historical novels, all illustrated in whole or in part by Cruikshank. The first three, *Jack Sheppard, Guy Fawkes*, and *The Tower of London*, were first published in the *Miscellany*; the second three, *The Miser's Daughter, Windsor Castle*, and *St. James: Or The Court of Queen Anne*, were first published in *Ainsworth's Magazine*, a monthly started by the author in January 1842 after breaking with Bentley. Cruikshank's relationships with both author and publisher were fraught with difficulties from this point on. The problems with Bentley started with the great success of *Jack Sheppard*, which brought about the usual dispute between the publisher, who was reaping the profits, and the author and artist, who were limited to their agreed-upon fees. In November, the parties reached an agreement whereby Ainsworth and Cruikshank would complete the next novel, *Guy Fawkes*, under Bentley's original terms, in return for which Bentley agreed to publish their next work, *The Tower of London*, for one-half net profits, the other half going to the author and artist, together with the copyrights. Cruikshank was ecstatic. He and Ainsworth would finally share in the fruits of their labors.[41]

However, disillusionment quickly set in. Acrimonious disputes over Bentley's accountings for the *Tower* partnership began early and continued before, during, and after publication. The expense reports of author and illustrator, delegated to Cruikshank, were messy and often late. The publisher's accountings showed little or no profit. In sum, while *The Tower of London* was a great success in the marketplace, it was a financial disaster for author and artist. Moreover, in the midst of Cruikshank's work on *Guy Fawkes* and *The Tower of London*, perhaps

---

40. During the 1820s, steel began to replace copper as the preferred medium for illustration by commercial publishers; and by the mid-1830s, it generally replaced copper in creating etchings for books and journals. A copperplate, being soft, allowed a freer but thicker line, and demanded a simpler form of design than the hard steel, but could be used to strike only a few hundred copies before the image began to deteriorate. The hardness of steel allowed the engraver to draw much finer, more detailed lines with more subtle tonal effect, and the resulting plate permitted press runs in the thousands. Cruikshank's mastery of both mediums can be seen by comparing his 1824 plates for Grimms Brothers' fairy tales with the plates for his 1854 *Cruikshank's Fairy Library*. Both are equally masterful, but quite different in tone, design, and detail.

41. This paragraph is a condensed version of the facts found in Patten, *George Cruikshank's Life*, 2:129–131.

irked by their new agreement, Bentley piled additional obligations on him for the *Miscellany*, and then complained about the quality of his plates and started hiring other artists (primarily John Leech and Alfred Crowquill) in violation of Cruikshank's role as the magazine's exclusive illustrator. Finally, in October 1843, weary of the disputes and Cruikshank's resentment, Bentley dismissed him.

Worse was Cruikshank's falling out with Ainsworth. In late 1840, publishers were clamoring for a sequel to *The Tower of London*. Indeed, one had approached Cruikshank with a proposal for the partnership's next book. However, without consulting his partner, Ainsworth sold to the *Sunday Times* a story based on the Great Fire of London that he and Cruikshank had discussed as their next joint project. Obviously, when he discovered what had happened, Cruikshank felt betrayed. However, since *Old Saint Paul's: A Tale of the Plague and the Fire* had been serialized in the newspaper without illustrations, Cruikshank hoped that Ainsworth would honor their partnership and ask him to illustrate the book. But the author delayed. So when Charles Tilt and his young partner, David Bogue, approached him in early 1841 about launching his own magazine, Cruikshank, relieved of his exclusive relationship with Bentley and undercut by Ainsworth, took up the project. Shortly thereafter, Dickens asked him if he would collaborate on an annual to be published by Chapman and Hall, which seems to have entailed an illustrated Christmas volume. Cruikshank, judging that he had gone too far with Tilt and Bogue to renege on his new monthly magazine, reluctantly turned Dickens down.[42]

George Cruikshank's Omnibus, edited by Laman Blanchard and published by Tilt & Bogue in May 1841, lasted less than a year. In a pattern that would follow, while many of the etchings are delightful, the written contributions are unmemorable. Indeed, Cruikshank opens the first issue with an eight-page diatribe, entitled "My Portrait," in which he complains at length about the physical description of him by James Grant in a recent book, *Portraits of Public Character*. While he attempts to write in a jocular manner, the lengthy description of his own physique projects only the bitterness of a middle-aged, would-be warrior longing for the compliments of his youth.

In December 1841, Ainsworth resigned as editor of *Bentley's Miscellany* and asked Cruikshank to help him create a new monthly. Cruikshank agreed and shut down his limping magazine. The first issue of *Ainsworth's Magazine* was published a month later with a cover designed by Cruikshank and the first installment of Ainsworth's next novel, *The Miser's Daughter*, illustrated with George's steel etchings. The book edition was published by Cunningham and Mortimer in late 1842 and was successful enough to be dramatized by two different London playwrights, with scenery based on Cruikshank's etchings. However, for his next book, *Windsor Castle*, on the death of Anne Boleyn, Ainsworth asked the famous French illustrator Tony Johannot to provide the plates. When Johannot quit after five plates, Cruikshank was called in and, again in need of commissions, he swallowed his pride and worked enthusiastically to make the publication a success. Finally, in the middle of publishing his next and final novel, *St. James: Or the*

42. Ibid., 2:162, 163. The first of Dickens's Christmas books, *A Christmas Carol*, published by Chapman and Hall in 1843, was illustrated by John Leech. Might George have become the illustrator of one or more of these small Christmas treasures if he had accepted Dickens's offer of collaboration?

Court of Queen Anne, Ainsworth, who was independently wealthy, but like Cruikshank no businessman, sold the unprofitable magazine to Mortimer, who became its publisher. Ainsworth had paid Cruikshank well; Mortimer promised to be stingy. So in 1845, the artist severed his relationships with both the magazine and Ainsworth.

Thus, as Cruikshank had less leverage as the years went on, his commissions were even more at the mercy of author and publisher. The success of Ainsworth's novels was unquestionably due in no small part to Cruikshank's creative ideas and fine steel etchings. But once successful, like Dickens, the author assumed himself to be chiefly responsible, and thoughtlessly dealt with the works for his own benefit without regard for the artist's well-being. Patten notes another negative aspect of Cruikshank's relationship with Ainsworth:

> The collaborations with Ainsworth were unfortunately proving that greatly superior plates depreciated the letterpress; the resultant books gradually disappeared from dealers' inventory. An artist who outstrips his author may end up eclipsing his own illustrations.

Once his work with Ainsworth ceased, Cruikshank sought to revitalize his own magazine, trying once more to make use of what he thought was the selling power of his own name and pencil, and to rid himself of the tyranny of authors and publishers. *George Cruikshank's Table Book* appeared at the end of 1844, edited by Gilbert Abbott à Beckett and published by Bradbury and Evans (the new owners and printers of *Punch*). The steel etchings were fine, but like *Omnibus*, the publication lasted only a year. For the next few years, Cruikshank continued to search for a niche that he could fill with his drawings without the need of writer or editor, but now with more of a story line than found in his whimsical albums of the 1820s and early 1830s, and with a more purposeful tone. *The Bachelor's Own Book; or The Progress of Mr. Lambkin, (Gent.), in the Pursuit of Pleasure and Amusement, and also in Pursuit of Health and Happiness,* published by David Bogue in 1844,[43] was a Hogarthian tale about the rise and fall of a young man yearning to be accepted in society. And in 1847 and 1848, Cruikshank teamed up with Henry Mayhew and his brother, Augustus, to publish three books of humorous morality tales also funded and published by his loyal friend Bogue.

Another crucial turning point in Cruikshank's career resulted from his decision to distance himself from the new humorous weekly, first published in July 1841. Clearly, the arrival of *Punch*, full of fresh faces in London's world of humorous publications, hastened the demise of Cruikshank's *Omnibus*, launched only two months earlier. What a pity that a man who had led a personal and professional life so full of jollity, collaboration, and collegiality should turn his back so disdainfully on the entreaties of talented younger colleagues that he join their happy endeavor. But that is what happened. It probably changed the future character of *Punch* as much as the future of Cruikshank's career.

Punch was founded by two of Cruikshank's colleagues, journalist and playwright Henry Mayhew (1812–1887) and wood engraver and illustrator Ebenezer Landells (1808–1860).[44] The

---

43. In 1841, Charles Tilt had retired from his partnership with David Bogue, leaving Bogue as sole owner.

44. The original title was *Punch or The London Charivari*, in reference to Charles Philipon's *Le Charivari*, which started in 1832. Mayhew had lived in Paris for a number of years, along with Thackeray, so both were well acquainted with Philipon's daily, featuring the famous lithographs of Honoré Daumier and others.

magazine was not immediately successful, Landells's rather awkward drawings comprising most of the initial illustrations. But sales gained traction as the writers picked up the pace and Leech became its principal artist. Initially, Mayhew and fellow journalist and playwright Mark Lemon (1809–1870) were co-editors, but Mayhew soon withdrew, leaving Lemon as sole editor, where he would serve for almost 30 more years. At the very outset, Lemon approached his close friend Cruikshank urging him to join the magazine on his own terms.[45] But Cruikshank adamantly and theatrically refused, and continued to refuse all subsequent appeals.[46]

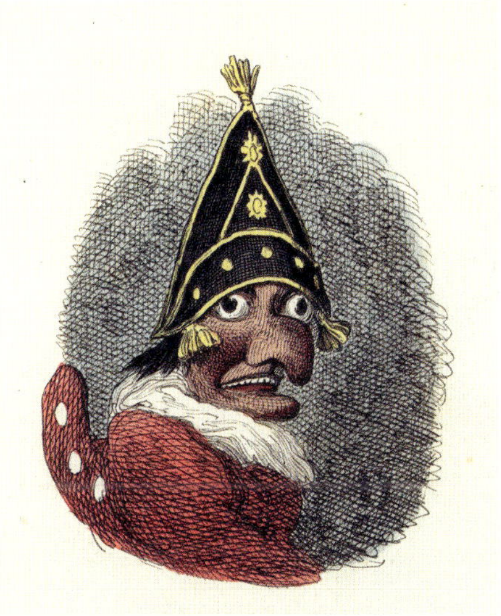

ITEM NO. 44

What prevailed upon Cruikshank to turn his back on *Punch*? Clearly he was a proud man, accustomed to being the leading artist in any publication, unaccustomed to sharing the spotlight. He had always been intent on guarding an artistic reputation that he seemed to believe was superior to the younger generation of humorists, particularly the new star, John Leech.[47] By mid-1841, he also may not have come to grips with the different role that an illustrator now played in collaborating with publishers and writers. To the contrary, he had been stung by these collaborations and may well have feared being hurt again. Lastly, Cruikshank, probably the most skilled engraver of the last three decades, had often etched and engraved his own designs. Thus, he may not have wanted to yield to the new protocol by which most of the next generation of artists would draw and an engraver would put those drawings on wood or steel. It is also worth noting that his wife, Mary Ann, was increasingly ill during this period, a grave

---

45. M. H. Spielmann, *The History of "Punch"* (New York: The Cassell Publishing Co., 31, East 17th Street (Union Square), 1895), 495, writes:

> Cruikshank was on terms of intimacy with Mark Lemon, but he never drew for *Punch*, save indirectly for its advertisement page in 1844 – an announcement for his *"Table Book,"* . . . Yet the *Quarterly Review* . . . declared that "*Punch* owes at least half its popularity to the pencil of George Cruikshank"! The fact is that Cruikshank, though on intimate terms with many of the Staff, would never allow himself to be persuaded to draw for its pages.

46. Cruikshank thumbed his nose at the new weekly in 1844 by publishing a third edition of his 1828 *Punch and Judy*, retitled *Punch's Real History, With Twenty-Eight Illustrations, Drawn and Engraved By George Cruikshank. Accompanied By the Tragical Comedy or Comical Tragedy of Punch and Judy; The Explanation of the Puppet-Show and Account of It's Origin*, published by Thomas Tegg, conveniently failing to give the name of the author, John Collier, on the title page.

47. Spielmann, *History of "Punch,"* 496, reports the following thoughts on the relationship between Cruikshank and Leech expressed by their contemporary, William Powell Frith, a Victorian painter who was also Leech's biographer:

> Between Cruikshank and Leech . . . there existed little sympathy and less intimacy. The extravagant caricature that pervades so much of Cruikshank's work, and from which Leech was entirely free, blinded him a little to the great merit of Cruikshank's serious work. I was very intimate with 'Immortal George' as he was familiarly called, and I was much surprised by the coolness with which he received my enthusiastic praise of Leech. . . . Nevertheless, it must not be forgotten that the only lessons in etching Leech ever had he received from George Cruikshank.

worry in and of itself, but to a man of modest means an increased financial burden that may have clouded his judgment. In any event, Patten draws the following conclusions from these various vicissitudes of George's career during the 1840s:

> In refusing to join *Punch*, in not working further with Dickens, in tying himself to second-rate writers such as Laman Blanchard and Gilbert à Beckett, in depending on niche publishers like Tilt & Bogue or Cunningham and Mortimer, Cruikshank slips from preeminence to mere eminence – not a major slide, but since his finances and artistic opportunities were always precarious, a difficult one to stop or reverse.[48]

The most useful and cheery chronicle of Cruikshank's work during the mid-1840s is provided by the faithful *Comic Almanack*. There one finds Cruikshank in full use of his old witty skills, but with a sharper pen depicting folk in perpetual conflict. Many issues of the day are attacked with humor: speculation on railroad shares; the horror of women with any serious thoughts other than hearth and home; and the usual rowdiness of social parties where drink is a boon, but then a bust. In the various depictions of the inebriated, there is no indication of disapproval at this point, only making fun of the ridiculous results that can occur from overindulgence. Several plates, however, indicate that temperance was becoming an accepted subject for discussion and was much on Cruikshank's mind. For example, the plate for January 1844, entitled "Wine versus Water," prefaces an amusing article entitled "The Great Anti-Temperance Meeting" attended by many bottles of assorted liquor haranguing against those preaching for water. And in September 1844, Cruikshank introduces abstinence in the form of a tall, London water pump in which the pump arrives at a dinner party and lectures the guests about the horrors of alcohol, to be shouted down by one and all.

1847–1850: THE ROAD TO TEMPERANCE

A highly convivial social drinker for many years, by the mid-1840s, Cruikshank was often drunk. Influenced by his own physical deterioration, financial distress, and the stress the situation must have placed on his ill wife, in 1846, the artist took up a suggestion of a Manchester reformer that he design and publish a series of drawings to promote temperance. He set to the project with enthusiasm and, hoping to reach the greatest audience possible, prepared eight etchings by the new method of glyphography,[49] depicting with realistic pathos the downfall of a working-class man and his family as the result of his obsession. *The Bottle* was published in 1847 by David Bogue in album form, the only text being Cruikshank's own subtitles. It was a serious Hogarthian morality tale, the work of the real artist that Cruikshank longed to be considered, and was a huge success, selling more than 100,000 copies in a few days, finding markets in America and Australia, and dramatized at

48. Patten, *George Cruikshank's Life*, 2:154. Maidment records an even more disparaging assessment of Gilbert à Beckett, concluding: "À Beckett was a famously hyperactive but, with the possible exception of *Figaro in London*, seldom a successful progenitor of periodicals of every kind." Maidment, "The Draughtman's Contacts," 49–50.
49. Glyphography, developed in the late 1830s as a form of etching, used a layer of wax over a hard metal plate on which the artist would engrave. A positive plate would then be created through stereotyping, allowing the image to be printed in relief with letterpress, speeding up the printing process and permitting a much longer press run.

eight London theaters simultaneously.[50] A sequel, *The Drunkard's Children,* was published by Bogue the following year.

As the result of a fateful meeting at this time, Cruikshank signed a pledge to join the temperance movement. As told by Jerrold, prior to its publication, the artist took proofs of his *Bottle* etchings to Mr. William Cash, then Chairman of the National Temperance Society, in hopes of gaining the support of his powerful organization. Mr. Cash, a Quaker, much taken with the pathos of the series, asked Cruikshank if he was an abstainer. When George had to admit that he indulged occasionally, the great man asked how he could have prepared such a moving case for the cause yet continue to take of the evil alcohol. On returning home, Cruikshank "resolv[ed] to give his example as well as his art to the total abstainers."[51] Wynn Jones tells the same story, adding insightful analysis of George's fateful decision:

> George liked to invest his irrevocable decisions with an air of theatricality (as he had done in the *Punch* office). Simply to renounce alcoholic beverages was too negative a gesture for one of his temperament: from the moment he decided to forswear drink George was, in effect, committed to the advancement of the Cause. . . . The Temperance Movement may not have lacked for orators, but it certainly was in need of artists: here was a focus not just for his energies, but also for his art. . . . At the age of fifty-five his horizons were narrowing: the celebrated authors he had once worked with continued to write without his assistance, his own journalistic creations had been virtually still-born. To George, as to many others in the late 1840s, the young Temperance Movement had all the hallmarks of the Establishment of the future. This was the way ahead.[52]

Notwithstanding *The Bottle*'s success, the next year brought Cruikshank tragedy. After a long illness, Mary Ann died of tuberculosis in May 1849. George collapsed with grief and under intense financial stress. His banker with whom he had deposited all his savings from *The Bottle*'s profits went bankrupt, leaving George with virtually nothing to pay substantial nursing bills, his ongoing expenses, and those of his brother Robert, who had been ill for some time and relied on George for the support of himself and his family. However, in March 1850, George married Eliza Widdeston, a widow in her mid-forties, niece of Charles Baldwyn, Cruikshank's early publisher. He moved from Amwell Street to Mornington Place with his new bride, together with his mother and Eliza's mother and aunt. Both of the latter died within 18 months, leaving Eliza a small inheritance that provided the couple with a modest degree of security.

Eliza was just what George needed at that point. Efficient and energetic, she kept meticulous financial records and acted as his assistant, writing letters on his behalf and keeping track of his plates. Most importantly, Eliza became George's most avid admirer (other than himself), protector-in-chief of his reputation, and determined to secure for them both a place in Victorian society for which they both longed.

---

50. Wynn Jones, *George Cruikshank: His Life,* 87.
51. Jerrold, *Cruikshank in Two Epochs,* 2:98, 99. George Dalziel and Edward Dalziel in their autobiography tell much the same story but relate that the fateful meeting was not with Mr. Cash, but with Dr. Blomfield, then Bishop of London. *The Brothers Dalziel, A Record of Fifty Years Work in Conjunction with Many of the Most Distinguished Artists of the Period 1840–1890* (London: Methuen and Co., 1902), 49–51.
52. Wynn Jones, *George Cruikshank: His Life,* 91.

1851–1878: THE SECOND EPOCH

Blanchard Jerrold entitled his 1882 biography of Cruikshank *The Life of George Cruikshank in Two Epochs* for good reason. The pre-Victorian George, product of Georgian London's streets and pubs, talented, successful, gay, quirky, generous, financially inept, disappears with Mary Ann's death and his remarriage to Eliza in 1850. "The Great George," then 58 years old, still a highly skilled and witty engraver, still quirky, generous but always indebted, was now a man energized principally by a passion for preaching abstinence, and a desperate need for recognition as an artist in Victorian society. An outline of the last 25 years of George's life is beyond the purview of this catalogue, except to say that, on the whole, it provides a rather depressing, detailed, and messy story – until one comes to the very end, when we learn of the ultimate and hidden contradiction of Cruikshank's long and eventful life.

In short, Cruikshank became a leader in the British temperance movement, theatrically proclaiming his own new health and vigor as propaganda for abstinence from alcohol and tobacco, and thriving on the attention he received from the committed. The accounts of his constant need for funds and indebtedness are tiresome; his desperate attempts to succeed as an oil painter are rather sad, since his prime motives appear to be fame and money. While he still produced many fresh and splendid etchings, many of his commissions involved re-etching works from his halcyon days, and attempts at large detailed oil paintings that were never quite as successful as he hoped. And then there were his odd quirky ventures, such as his appointment at age 67 as Colonel of the Havelock Volunteer Temperance Corps during a threat of French invasion, and a pet project involving the building of a national railroad for Turkey. A description here of two more of Cruikshank's works will provide a rather sad coda to the first epoch of his life, and a bittersweet preface to the second.

Coda to the First Epoch: *1851: or The Adventures of Mr. and Mrs. Sandboys and Family*

The Victorian era came into full flower just at this time with the Great Exhibition of 1851. The first international industrial exhibition ever held was the creation of Henry Cole and Prince Albert.[53] It was a natural to attract Cruikshank's strong interest. As described by Patten:

> This quintessentially Victorian marriage of commercialism, aesthetics and social engineering seemed to promise a new era for industrialism, one in which the worker became an artisan, a craftsman who imbued the product of his labor with a beauty and individuality that transformed repetitive, mechanical work into a noble, spiritually expressive activity. . . . As an etcher who experimented with new reproductive processes, [Cruikshank] could empathize with the plight of innovative workers debarred from the higher reaches of art by time-honored prejudices; after all, no engraver or etcher had yet been admitted to membership in the Royal Academy. . . . And the connection to the crown placed the festival under the same patronage he was beginning to receive

53. Henry Cole (1808–1882), who with Prince Albert's support had organized prior industrial exhibitions, was instrumental in creating the Royal Commission for the Exhibition of 1851 to manage the new exhibition under the Presidency of the Prince Regent. Wikipedia, s.v. "Henry Cole," accessed April 2, 2020, https://en.wikipedia.org/wiki/Henry Cole.

for his paintings.[54] Cruikshank could envisage a new era for his art, wherein he would collaborate with the highest ranks to change the habits and improve the lives of the common people.[55]

1851: or The Adventures of Mr. and Mrs. Sandboys and Family Who Came Up to London to Enjoy Themselves and to See the Great Exhibition was a collaboration between Cruikshank and Henry Mayhew, in which they followed the Sandboys family from Manchester to London with all the jolly adventures that that might entail. It was classic social satire of country bumpkins in the big capital, with the Crystal Palace, crowds, and foreigners thrown in. The work was first published by David Bogue in eight parts from February through October 1851, intended to span the excitement building up to the grand opening by the Queen on May 1 and lasting through its closing and massive dispersal in October. Mayhew was paid an upfront fee per part for the text, while Bogue and Cruikshank were equal partners in profits or losses. In theory, the series was a perfect vehicle for the wit and skills of our hero. However, Mayhew was not up to the job. His writing fell flat, telling a rather incoherent story; he produced copy late or not at all. Despite some initially fine steel plates (as the series flagged, Cruikshank's etchings visibly deteriorated), the series was a terrible financial failure, leaving the publisher with substantial debts, a large portion of which would be charged to Cruikshank after Bogue's death in 1856.[56] Once again, the artist suffered by not being able to team up with a first-class author to carry out this potentially wonderful contribution to Victoriana.

Preface to the Second Epoch: George Cruikshank's Fairy Library

In the fall of 1852, Cruikshank, anxious to generate income, turned back to the source of some of his greatest successes: fairies, giants, and witches. Rather than hiring a writer to retell familiar tales, he decided to do the "editing" himself, and persuaded Bogue to advance him funds to finance the project. The first of the four tales eventually to form *George Cruikshank's Fairy Library* was *Hop-O'-My-Thumb and the Seven-League Boots*. Published in June 1853 as a small book in a blue paper wrapper with a delightful Cruikshankian engraved design, *Hop* was filled with fanciful steel etchings, some of Cruikshank's very best, and initially sold well to admiring critics and delighted parents. Little was noted of the fact that Cruikshank's written version of the tale was filled with temperance propaganda.

Dickens, however, quickly took note, and publicly at that. As a result, a duel of polite words that had been simmering for some time between the artist and the writer on the subject of temperance[57] boiled over into a rancorous dispute that permanently severed their dwindling friendship. Dickens had grown more and more averse to the temperance movement as its fanaticism and influence in England grew. In the fall of 1851, in response to a number of ral-

---

54. In 1849, Prince Albert had purchased one of Cruikshank's early oil paintings. Patten, *George Cruikshank's Life,* 2:289.
55. Ibid., 2:294. It should be noted that all alcohol was banned from the Great Exhibition, the temperance movement having gained much support from Prince Albert.
56. Ibid., 2:297–306, 352.
57. Both were reformers. But Dickens's focus was on relief of poverty by social justice and education reform. He favored temperance, not abstinence. Cruikshank, on the other hand, firmly adopted the radical view of the National Temperance League. Alcohol was the source of all social evils. Total abstinence was the only path.

ITEM NO. 85A

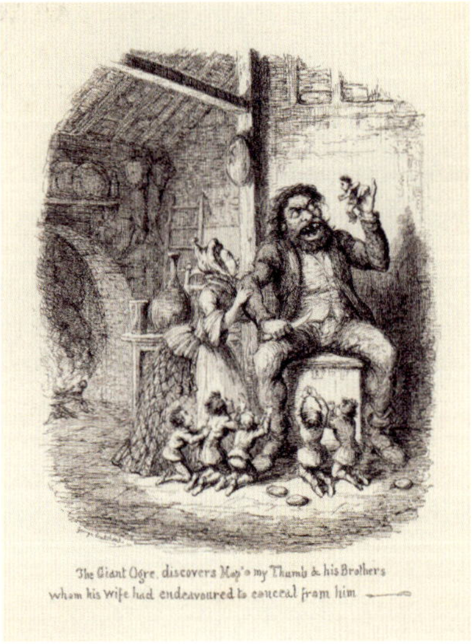

lies conducted during the Great Exhibition in the name of temperance, he wrote a lengthy satirical piece in his magazine, *Household Words,* entitled *Whole Hog,* making fun in sharp critical terms of the movement, particularly targeting the American movement from which Britain's counterparts seemed to be drawing much inspiration. Two years later, a few months after *Hop* was published, Dickens exploded again with a scathing critique of the fairy tale, entitled "Fraud on the Fairies," published in *Household Words*. In it, he attacked Cruikshank personally for misusing and mistelling the old beloved fairy tale for propaganda purposes.

Cruikshank, baffled and enraged by this onslaught from a man whom he considered his friend and collaborator in the cause of reform, fired back "A Letter from Hop-O'-My-Thumb to Mr. Charles Dickens, Esq.," published in February 1854 in the second issue of *George Cruikshank's Magazine* (his third and final attempt to sustain a monthly magazine that he could edit and illustrate himself). Hop takes up his pen "made from the quill of a hummingbird" to defend his editor (Cruikshank) and set the famous author straight about his family's true story and the true nature of the fairy tale:

> These may seem bold words, from such a mite as I am to such a literary giant as you are; but I have had to deal with giants in my time, and I am not afraid of them, and I shall therefore take leave to tell you, that although you may have held in your memory some of the remarkable facts in my interesting history, yet that you were ignorant of the general character of the whole; and the only way I can account for the way in which a man of your remarkable acuteness making such a great mistake, is, that you have suffered that extraordinary seven-league boot imagination of yours to run away with you into your *own* Fairy Land, – and thus have given your *own* colour to this history; and consequently a credit and a character to the old editions, which do not belong to them.[58]

Cruikshank's passion for his new cause had intruded into fairyland, and once the famous author had drawn attention to the temperance stranger in the text and made poisonous fun of it, sales of *Hop* faded. Cruikshank, deaf to the effect of his "editing," battled on in the same vein, producing *Cinderella and the Glass Slipper* and *The History of Jack & the Bean-Stalk* in 1854, also published by Bogue, also turning each into a temperance tract.[59] Once again, the illustrations created by the artist would be sacrificed because of the author. This time, however, the author was Cruikshank himself. It appears that he never could understand the isolation into which he had barricaded himself from the artistic circles of London's society, of which he so longed to be a part, by his unwavering and tiresome lecturing in the cause of temperance.

---

58. An eight-page reprint of Cruikshank's "A Letter from Hop-O'-My-Thumb to Charles Dickens, Esq. Upon 'Frauds on the Fairies,' 'Whole Hog,' &c.," published and distributed in pamphlet form by David Bogue in 1854, Price One Pence, pp. 1, 2. See Item No. 86.

59. The fourth tale included in *Cruikshank's Fairy Library*, *Puss in Boots*, was published by Routledge, Warne, and Routledge in 1864.

EPILOGUE

At George's death on January 31, 1878, there was an outpouring of obituaries, tributes, articles, and incipient biographies for the grand old man.[60] In his *Critico-Biographical Essay* on the life of George Cruikshank, published only months after the artist's death, the literary critic, surgeon, and Cruikshank collector William Bates wrote: "[Britain] in its comparatively brief art-life has already produced four great typical masters of Pictorial Satire [Hogarth, Gillray, Rowlandson and George Cruikshank]." Among the four, he makes the closest comparison between Hogarth and Cruikshank:

> We now come to George Cruikshank, . . . the last of our quarternion, – if not the line of purely comic artists, – the *omega*, as Hogarth was the *alpha* – of satirical designers. Handing down the fire of national humour in direct descent from that great master, he too essayed the whole dramatic field; and thus a comparison is suggested, which, if pushed too far, is unfair to both. For the genius of the one differs from that of the other in kind as well as degree; and there is little resemblance in the circumstances of their lives. Hogarth had the advantage of a thorough early training; Cruikshank picked up his art when and how he could. The one has left us elaborate works, the result of deliberate thought and careful execution; the other a vast number of trivial designs . . . born of occasion and spontaneous impulse, redeemed and exalted alone by the informing art. . . . [I]f the later artist is inferior to the earlier when he comes into direct competition with him, he has reached the highest excellence in certain peculiar walks of his own. In the depiction of low, vicious and vulgar life, – in the ridiculous, and the quaint, the weird, the pathetic, and the terrible, – he is unsurpassed. No one has touched with a nicer humour the manners of his day, and the frivolities and affectations of fashionable life; no one so felicitously illustrated the mysteries of folk-lore and popular superstition. Like Hogarth, he possessed a supreme faculty of graphic narration, and an unerring tact in the seizure of dramatic incident.[61]

Patten winds up his assessment of the artist with a brief, but interesting, observation of Cruikshank's deep influence on the English and French artists of the 19th century:

> His art, though increasingly out of favor, had in countless ways soaked into the roots of nineteenth century European culture and influenced its flowering. Every black-and-white draftsman, from Robert Seymour and John Leech to John Gilbert, George Du Maurier and Randolph Caldecott, learned something from his examples. Whistler and Sickert considered Cruikshank the greatest nineteenth century English artist. On the Continent, two generations of French artists imitated aspects of his work: Monnier, Gericault, Delacroix, Daumier, Grandville, Gavarni, Doré.[62]

In retrospect, however, the most intriguing aspect of George Cruikshank's Second Epoch surfaced, in a most public manner, in his will. As the ultimate contradiction to the highly respectable life of Victorian rectitude he had adopted with his wife Eliza, he left the bulk of his estate not to his wife, but in trust for the benefit of one "Adelaide Archibald, otherwise Ad-

---

60. See generally Patten, *George Cruikshank's Life,* 2:508, 509.

61. William Bates, B.A., M.R.C.S.E., Etc., *George Cruikshank: The Artist, The Humourist, and The Man, With Some Account of His Brother Robert. A Critico-Bibliographical Essay* (Birmingham, Houghton and Hammond, Scotland Passage, 1878), 1–3.

62. Patten, *George Cruikshank's Life*, 2:504. See also *Distractions* by Henry Monnier, dedicated to Cruikshank, Item No. 45.

elaide Altree" and her ten children, whose names and birthdates (ranging from 1854 to 1875) were specified in the will.[63] It appears that within months of his remarriage in 1850, he became attached to a young woman named Adelaide Altree who had entered the Cruikshanks' employ as a housemaid. She soon became pregnant, and apparently, George set up house for her at 31 Augustus Street, a few blocks from his marital home on Mornington Place.[64] While the obituaries, newspapers tributes, and contemporary biographies, out of Victorian reserve and respect, generally took pains to avoid this aspect of the artist's life,[65] it appears that, right around the corner from "home," George had supported a mistress and sired and maintained a large and boisterous family, where he enjoyed hearth, home, and a second studio for the second epoch of his life. No wonder he was in constant financial stress.

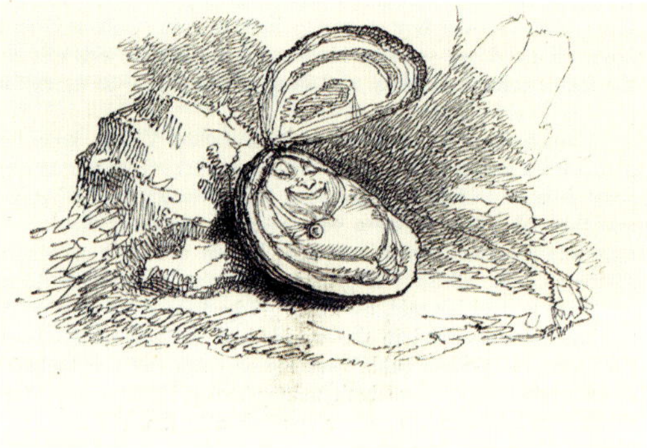

ITEM NO. 47

63. The will provided that all prints, drawings, plates, and artwork of any kind located in the Cruikshank marital home were to be sold and the net proceeds, along with other assets in the estate, managed in trust for Adelaide for her lifetime, and at her death were to be divided equally among her ten named children. Eliza worked for many years after George's death to clear the estate from its myriad debts and to sell the remainder of his works to realize funds for the trust set up for his mistress and children. Patten, *George Cruikshank's Life,* 2:514, 515.

64. See generally ibid., 2:286–288.

65. For example, neither William Bates in his 1878 biographical essay nor Blanchard Jerrold in his 1882 biography mentions these facts.

III

Prints, Original Drawings, and Documents

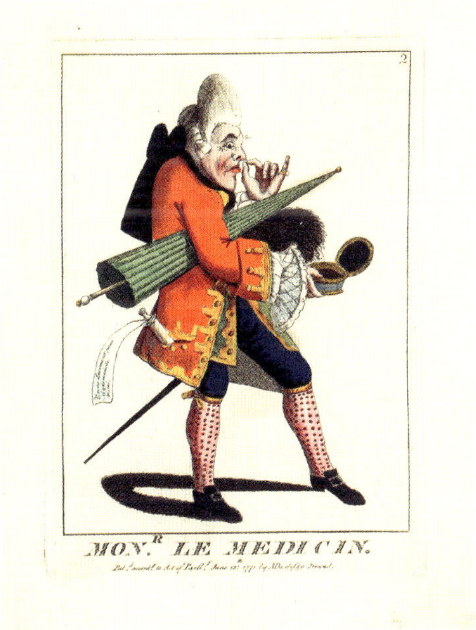

ITEM NO. 1.
Volume I, Plate 2: "Mon.r Le Medicin."

1792–1811:
BEGINNINGS: GEORGE'S EDUCATION IN THE ART OF HUMOR

I

24 Caricatures by Several Ladies. Gentlemen. Artists. &c. Pub'd. by MDarly. Strand. Pubd. by MDarly, Engraver, No 39 Strand according to Act Novr 1 1771. *Vol. II of Caricatures. Macaronies & Characters by Sundry Ladies. Gentle, Artist, &c.* Pub.d by MDarly. No. 39 Strand, 1772. The first two of six volumes of caricatures/macaronies published by Mary Darly from 1771 to 1773. Each of these volumes has 24 hand-colored engravings of characters from the London streets, a hand-colored engraved title page, and one leaf of engraved text. Several of the plates are signed by Henry Bunbery and other artists. In the mid-18th century, a macaroni was the term used for a well-traveled British young man who had been to Italy on the Grand Tour and returned to London dressed in high fashion with a taste for macaroni. Mary Darly, artist, engraver, and print-seller, was one of the first professional caricaturists in England. She wrote, illustrated, and published the first book on caricature drawing (*A Book of Caricaturas*, 1762). Mary and her husband, Matthew, owned a print shop in the fashionable West End of London that came to be known as the Macaroni Print-Shop.[66]

66. Rness. "The Martial Macaroni: Pray Sirs, Do You Laugh at Me?" *Curio* (blog of Digital Production Services, Brown University Library), August 21, 2013, https://library.brown.edu/dps/curio/tag/macaroni.

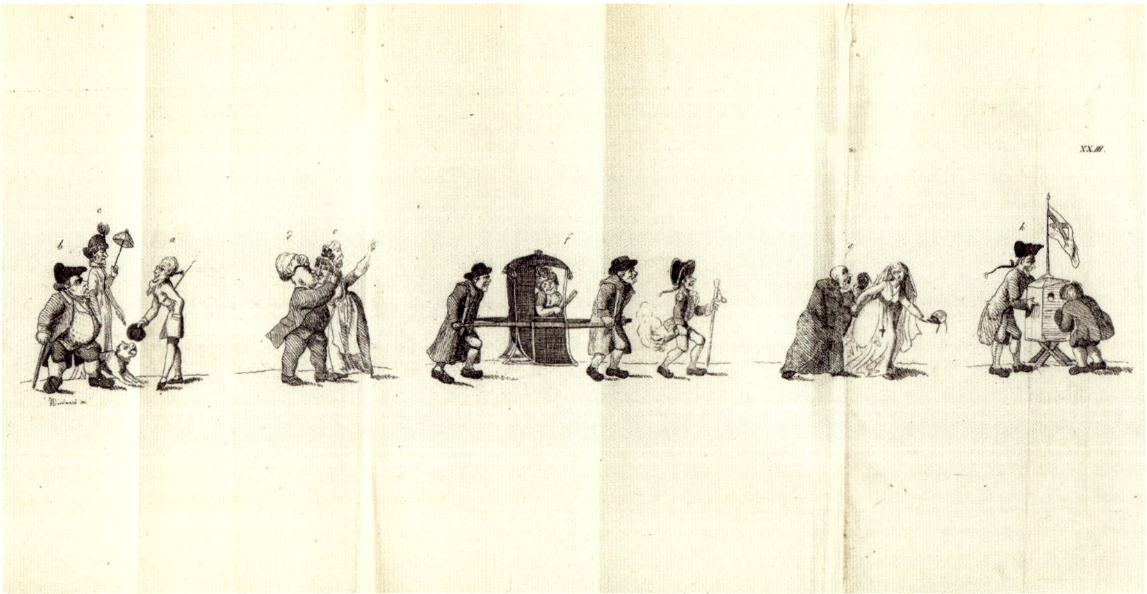

ITEM NO. 2. Plate XXIII. "Explications" [The legends are translated but not very funny.] abc "'Glad to see you here. Have you met our child [the dog]?' 'This is the first time I have seen him.' d&e 'I must kiss you one more time.' 'I'm calling my mistress, I'm telling you.' f An elegant lady in a porte-chaise. g 'What is this! It's my wife! Oh! You were too charming to have been a nun.' h The peep show."

2

Principes de Caricatures, suivis d'un Essai sur la Peinture Comique. par François Grose, Membre de la Société des Antiquités de Londrès. Traduits en français, avec des augmentations. À Paris, chez Antoine-Augustin Renouard. ANX – 1802. Engraved frontispiece (an amusing self-portrait by Grose) and 28 engraved black and white plates numbered I–XXVIII. The last six are each on a large folding paper containing a long line of small, amusing figures, each signed by "Woodward inv" [George M. Woodward]. The frontispiece and all but two of plates I–XXII are signed by F. Grose as designer and by F. G. Grohmann as engraver ("fecit"). Francis Grose (1731?–1791) was an English antiquarian, artist, lexicographer, and army captain. This book was first published in English in 1788; a second edition was published in French in Leipzig in 1800 with many more plates than in the original English edition, all of which are included in this edition.

3

Le Lavater Portatif, ou precis de l'art de connoitre [sic] des hommes par les traits du visage, avec trente-trois planches coloriées. Troisieme Edition. Paris, Chez Madame veuve HOCQUART, Libraire, Rue de l'Eperon, No. 6. 1809. Johann Caspar Lavater (1741–1801) was born and lived in Zurich. His multi-volume work on physiognomy, published in 1775–1778, was the foundation for much of the 19th-century British and French caricaturists' interest in physiognomy.

4

George Cruikshank: The Artist, the Humorist, and the Man, with Some Account of His Brother, Robert. A Critico-Biographical Essay. Illustrated Chiefly from Original Drawings by G. Cruikshank, in the Possession of the Author. By William Bates, B.A., R.C.S.E., Etc. Birmingham: Houghton and Hammond, 1878. EXTRA-ILLUSTRATED. There were 77 pages of printed text and 21 illustrations in the originally published work. This first edition has 263 additional engravings on copper, steel, and wood bound in. Most are by George Cruikshank, including some of his finest prints and two watercolors. There are also several early caricatures by Isaac Cruikshank, many works by brother Robert Cruikshank and his son, Percy, and others, including John Doyle's striking foldout, hand-colored print, "Funeral of Tory-principle" [Lord Wellington's funeral], published by Thos. McLean, 26 Haymarket, 1827.

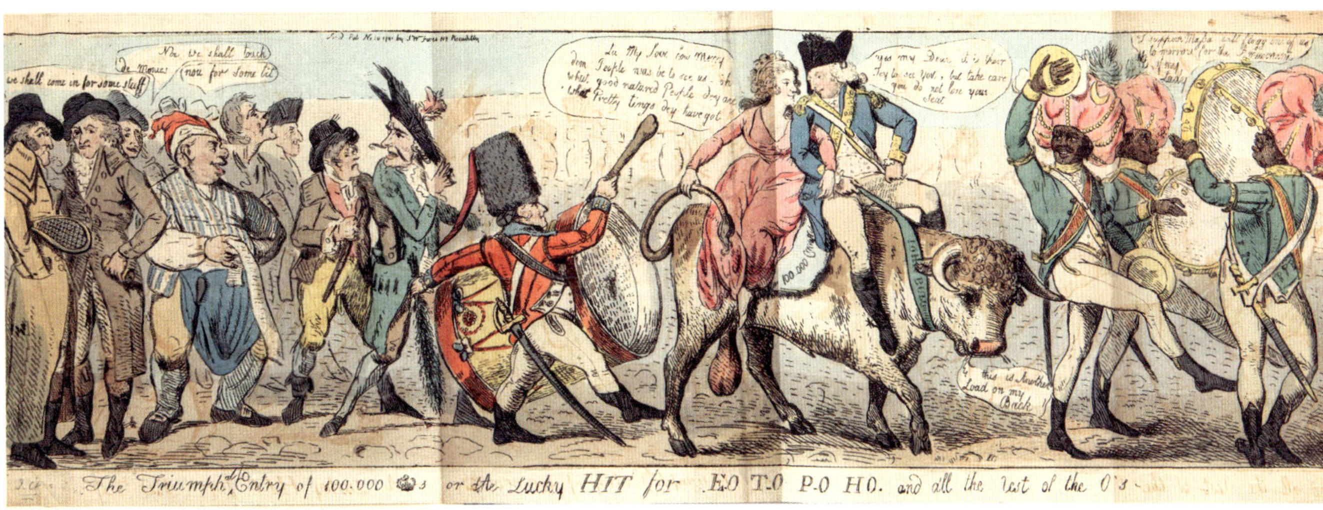

ITEM NO. 4A. "The Triumphal Entry of the 100,000 (crown')s or the lucky hit for e-o t-o p-o ho. and all the rest of the o's." Foldout, hand-colored etching signed "IC" [Isaac Cruikshank]. [Published by S. W. Fores, 20 November 1791]. A burlesque of the Duke and Duchess of York entering London. The Duke, Prince Frederick Augustus (1763–1827), George III's second son, had just married his cousin, Princess Frederica Charlotte, daughter of King Frederick William II of Prussia, in Berlin on 29 September 1791. They arrived in London on November 19, 1791, for a second marriage at Buckingham Palace on 23 November 1791. The pair sits on the back of John Bull (the ordinary English taxpayer) who moans, "This is another load on my back." The Duchess says, "La My Love how Merry dem People was be to see us. oh what good natured People dey are What Pretty tings dey have got." He answers, "yes My Dear it is their Joy to see You, but take care you do not lose your Seat." BMS 7903.*

ITEM NO. 4B. "The Cholic," [Anchor] [Frederick Marryat, del.] G. Cruikshank fecit. Publ by Thos. McLean, 26 Haymarket, Aug. 1, 1835. Second issue. First published February 12, 1819, by George Humphrey. See image on page 13.

ITEM NO. 4C. Stipple engraving by C. E. Wagstaff of self-portrait by George Cruikshank with signature. See Frontispiece.

* British Museum, and M. Dorothy George. *Catalogue of Political and Personal Satires Preserved in the Department of Prints and Drawings in the British Museum.* London: British Museum Publications, 1935–1954.

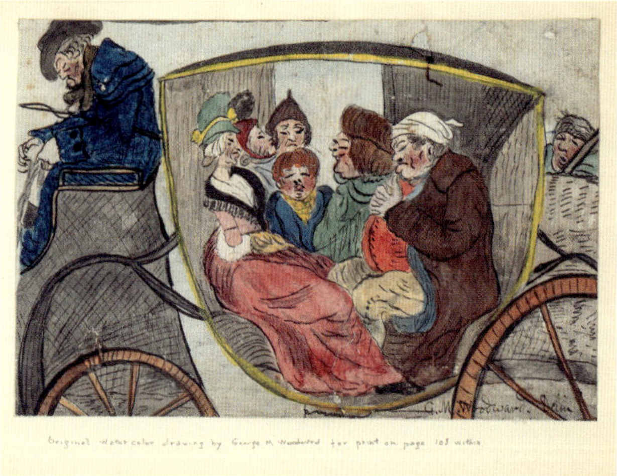

ITEM NO. 5A. Penciled legend: "Original watercolor drawing by George M. Woodward for print on page 103 within." Signed in black ink, "G.M. Woodward. Delin."

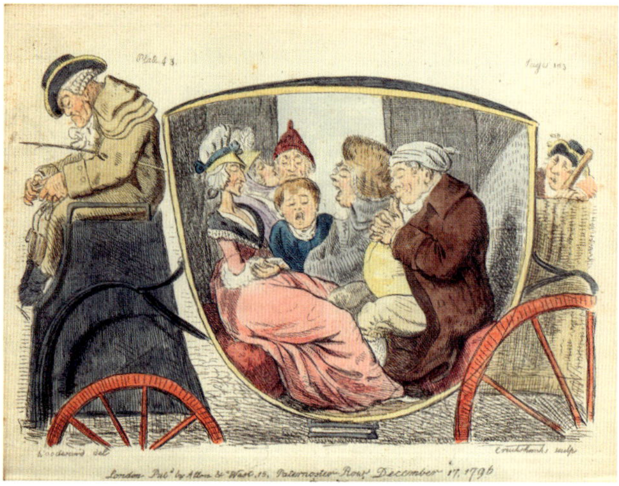

ITEM NO. 5B. Hand-colored etching on page 103: "Plate 43 Woodward, del. Cruikshank, sculp. London. Pubd. by Allen & West, 15, Paternoster Row, December 17, 1796."

5

Eccentric Excursions or Literary & Pictorial Sketches of Countenance, Character & Country, in different parts of England & South Wales. Interspersed with Curious Anecdotes. Embellished with upwards of One Hundred Characteristic & Illustrative Prints. By G. M. Woodward. Engraved by Isaac Cruikshank. London: Published by Allen & Co. 15 Paternoster Row. 1796. First edition with over 100 hand-colored plates engraved by Isaac Cruikshank after Woodward's drawings. Dedicated to William Woodward, Stanton Hall, Derbyshire [the author's father and birthplace].

6

Habits of New French Legislators and Other Public Functionaries, London. H. Humphrey, 1798. Album. Series of 12 hand-colored, numbered plates drawn and etched by James Gillray. These etchings satirize prominent Whigs of the day, most of whom had supported the revolutionary goals of the American and French revolutions. By 1798, the French Revolution had become bloody and unsupportable. The costume of the

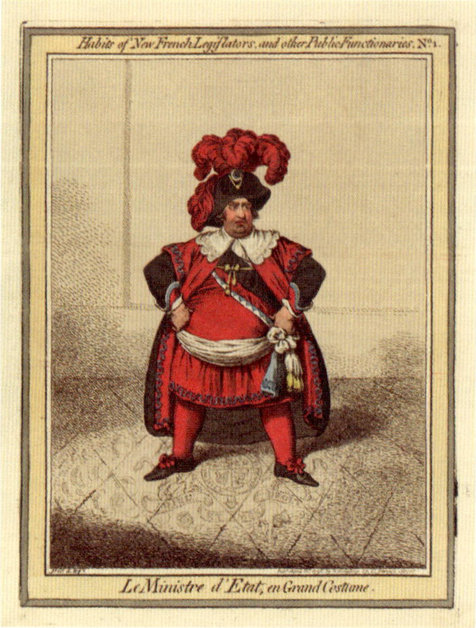

ITEM NO. 6. Plate No. 1: "Le Ministre d'Etat. En Grand Costume." [Mr. Fox]. Hand-colored engraving with aquatint. Js. Gy. d & f't. Publ. April 18, 1798 by H. Humphrey, 27 St. James Street. Charles James Fox (1749–1806) was a prominent Whig statesman and archrival of William Pitt the Younger, leader of the Tory party. He opposed war against the French advocated by Pitt in 1797. In May 1798, Pitt had Fox thrown out of the Privy Council because of his views.

officials of the Directory, designed by Jacques-Louis David, official painter to Napoleon, was regulated by a complementary law of the Constitution of the Year III, enacted the year these plates were engraved. BMS 9196.

7

New Pantheon of Democratic Mythology. London. H. Humphrey, May 7, 1799. Folio. Six hand-colored etchings drawn and etched by James Gillray.

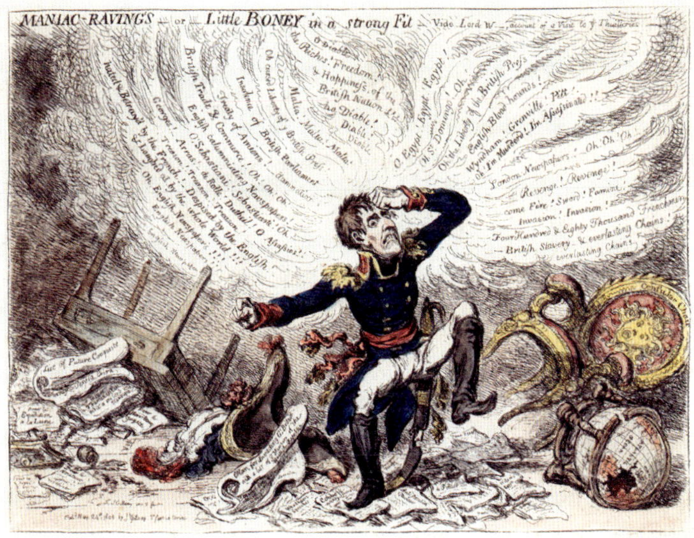

ITEM NO. 8

8

"Maniac Ravings or Little Boney in a Strong Fit —Vide. Lord W- account of a Visit to c/y Tuilleries." Hand-colored etching, Js Gillray invt & fect. Pubd May 24th 1803, by Js Gillray, St James Street. A burlesque of Napoleon's grievances against England. The print is making fun of the famous scene made by the First Consul at a levée on 13 March 1803, when he reproached John Whitworth, then British Ambassador to Paris, with the conduct of the British government. From Napoleon's head swirls the aspects of Britain causing him the most fury. As noted by Dorothy George, the texts written on Napoleon's brain storms and on the many documents strewn around the room show Gillray's detailed grasp of the political situation between France and England, as well as of Britain's internal politics at the time. BMS 7120.

9

Essay on the Art of Ingeniously Tormenting. A New Edition. Corrected, Revised and Illustrated with five Prints, from Designs by George M. Woodward, Esq.; etched by Th. Rowlandson. London: Printed by Thomas Tegg, 111, Cheapside; by Harard and Carthew, Breech-Street, 1808.

ITEM NO. 10. Foldout frontispiece.

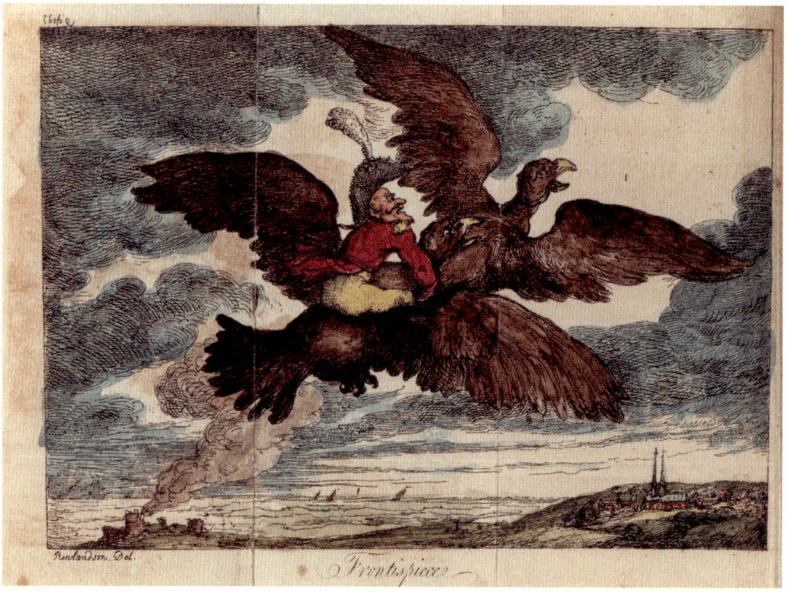

10

Surprising Adventures of Baron Munchausen, Containing Singular Travels, Campaign, Voyages, and Adventures. Also an Account of a Voyage to the Moon and Dog Star. Embellished with Numerous Engravings by Thomas Rowlandson. 1809. London: Printed for Thomas Tegg, No. 111, Opposite Bow Church, Cheapside.

11

The English Dance of Death, From the Designs of Thomas Rowlandson, with Metrical Illustrations, by the author of "Doctor Syntax" [William Combe]. London: Printed by J. Diggins, St. Ann's Lane; Published at R. Ackermann's Repository of Arts, 101, Strand; and to be had of all the Book and Print-sellers in the United Kingdom. Two Volumes. 1815, 1816. First book edition. EXTRA-ILLUSTRATED. 74 hand-colored aquatints with three additional hand-colored etchings before letters bound in. Originally published in parts. Rowlandson's contemporary version of the late-medieval allegory on the universality of death no matter one's station in life.

12

Doctor Syntax in London; or the Pleasures and Miseries of the Metropolis. A Poem. By Doctor Syntax. London: Published by J. Johnson, Cheapside. In eight Parts, I–VIII, each signed "Geo. Pountrey." By William Combe. "Both Rowlandson and I.R. Cruikshank are credited with the designs for the plates, the balance of opinion favoring Cruikshank but according to the advertisement more than one artist was employed, or at least a different engraver to the artist."[67]

---

67. R. V. Tooley, *English Books with Coloured Plates, 1790–1860, A Bibliographical Account of the Most Important Books Illustrated by English Artists in Colour Aquatint and Colour Lithography* (2d ed.). London: B. T. Batsford Ltd., 1954: 434.

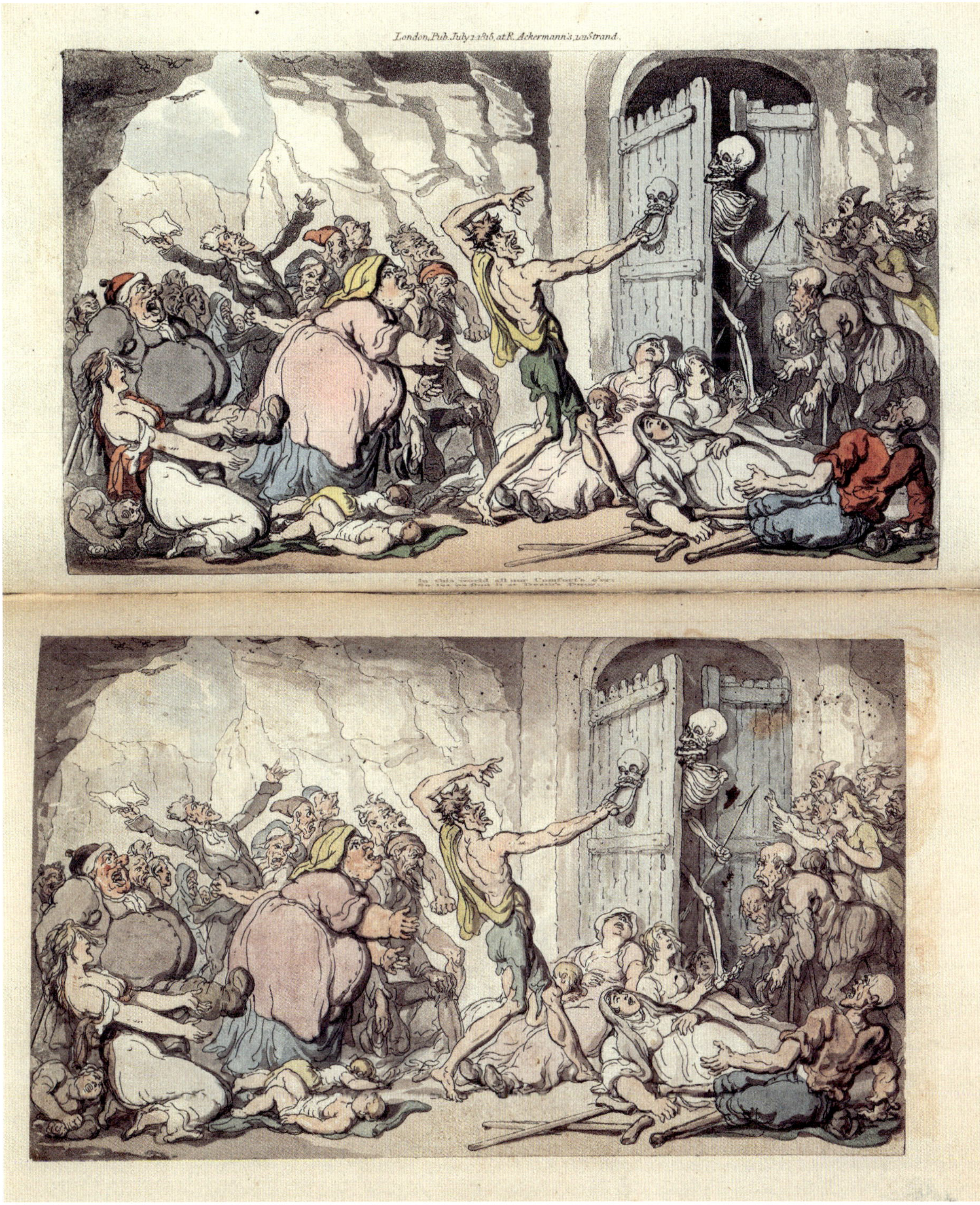

ITEM NO. 11. Volume 11, p. 101: "In this world Our Comfort's o'er, So let us find it at Death's Door." London. July 1, 1815 at R. Ackermann's, 101 Strand. Together with proof of same plate before letters.

13

"The Bear and Bear Leader." Original pen and sepia ink drawing and watercolor, signed in ink on lower right-hand corner of painting, "Rowlandson 1776," on Whatman paper dated 1816. Printed in pen and ink on the lower matte: "The Bear and Bear Leader / 1756 Thomas Rowlandson 1827" [Rowlandson's birth and death dates]. In the 18th and 19th centuries, a bear-leader was a colloquialism for a man who escorted young men of rank or wealth on their Grand Tour. Rowlandson was sent to Paris at age 16 to study at a drawing academy, and stayed for two years. Was the elderly artist making fun of himself being introduced to life in Paris as a teenager?

1811–1820: YOUNG GEORGE AS POLITICAL SATIRIST

14

The Scourge; or Monthly Expositor, of Imposture and Folly. Vols. I–VI. London: Printed by W. N. Jones, Green Arbor Court, Old Bailey; for M. Jones, 5 Newgate Street; and sold by J. Johnson, Cheapside, and Goddard Pall Mall. (1811–1813). In 1814, name changed to *The Scourge: or Literary, Theatrical and Miscellaneous Magazine*, London: Printed and Published by W. N. Jones, No. 5 Newgate Street, and Sold by all the Booksellers in the United Kingdom. Vols. VII–X (1814–1815). Vol. XI (Jan–June, 1816): printed and published by James Johnson.

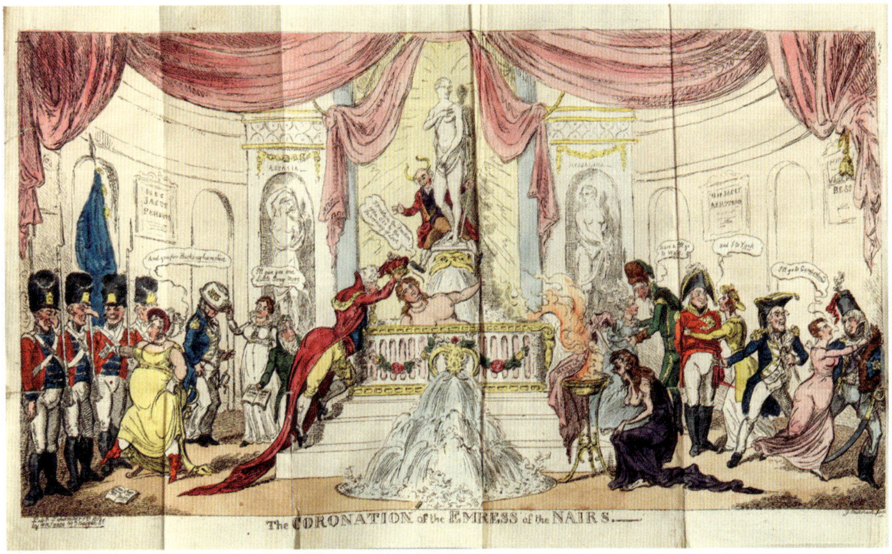

ITEM NO. 14A. Volume IV: "The Coronation of the Empress of the Nairs," Pubd. September 1, 1812 by WN Jones, No. 5 Newgate, G. Cruikshank fecit. Foldout, hand-colored etching referring to a recent romance by J. H. Lawrence, "The Empire of Nairs." BMS 12677. The Nairs were groups of Hindi castes that practiced polygamy and hypergamy (marrying above your social caste). Lady Hertford, Isabella Anne Seymour-Conway, Marchioness of Hertford (1759–1834), became mistress of the Prince of Wales in 1807. As a result, the Prince was a regular guest at Hertford's residences. She was influential in turning the Prince toward Tory causes.*

* Wikipedia, s.v. "Isabella Ingram-Seymour-Conway, Marchioness of Hertford," accessed June 19, 2020, https://en.wikipedia.org/wiki/Isabella_Ingram-Seymour-Conway,_Marchioness_of_Hertford.

Vol. XII (July–Dec. 1816): A new series entitled *The Scourge and Satirist; or Literary, Theatrical and Miscellaneous Magazine,* np. 12 volumes complete. Each month had a hand-colored engraved caricature, for a total of 77 hand-colored engraved and etched plates, including two copies of the suppressed plate, before and after censorship. Of the 77 plates, 73 are foldouts; George Cruikshank provided 42.

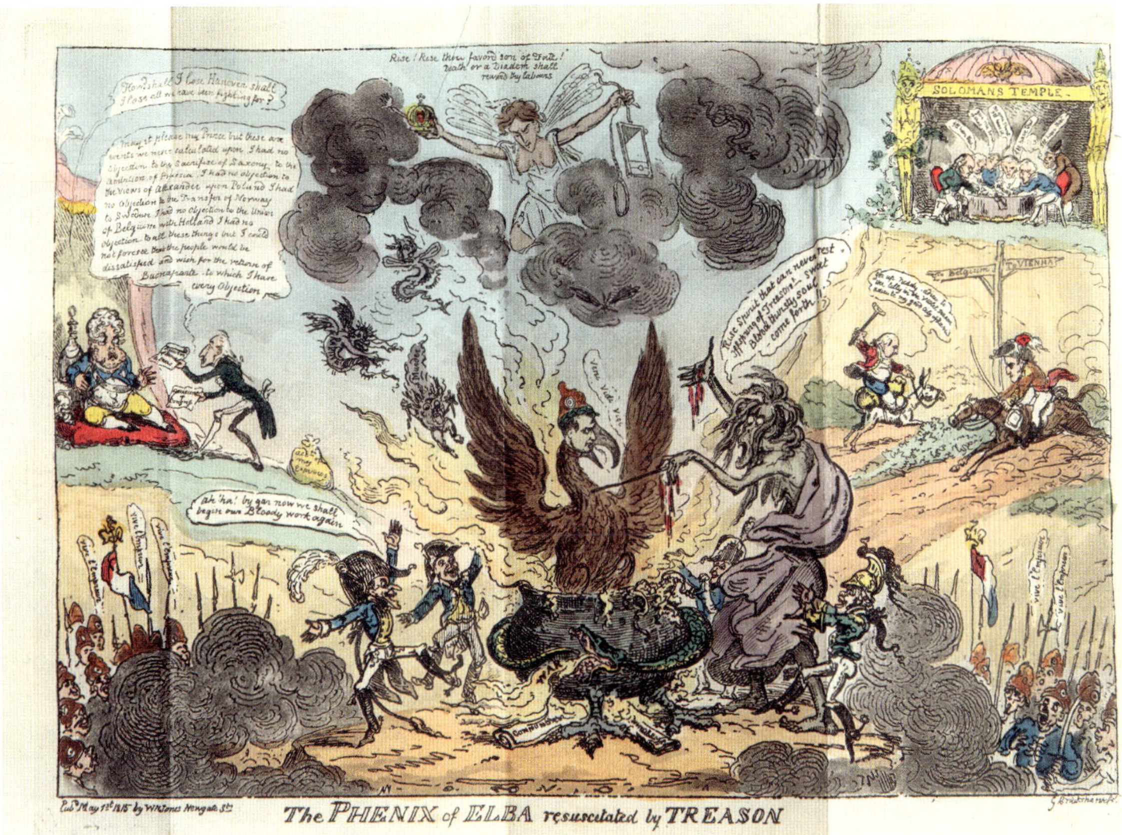

ITEM NO. 14B. Volume IX: "The Phoenix of Elba Resuscitated by Treason," Pubd. May 1, 1815 by WN Jones, Newgate. G. Cruikshank fecit. Foldout, hand-colored etching, the background of which was Napoleonic France's defeat and surrender in May 1814, followed by 18 months of negotiations at the Congress of Vienna to agree upon peace terms once Napoleon was defeated. Negotiations continued despite the outbreak of fighting triggered by Napoleon's dramatic return from exile in March. The Congress's "final act" was signed nine days before his final defeat at Waterloo on 18 June 1815. By May 1, when this print was published, there was great disagreement in Britain on whether to continue the war against France, and a strong distrust of the Regent and his Foreign Secretary, Lord Castlereagh, for having sided with England's conservative allies in dividing up the spoils of war at the expense of emerging national and liberal movements.* Here, Napoleon arises from the cauldron of war with his French army officers dancing in joy around the flames. Castlereagh is reporting to the Regent that he had had no objection to the terms of the peace treaty, but "I could not foresee that the people would be dissatisfied and wish for the return of Buonaparte, to which I have every Objection." Behind him is a large money-bag inscribed "Acct of my Expences." The Regent, with a gesture of alarm, answers: "How? Shall I lose Hanover? shall I lose all we have been fighting for?" BMS 8213.

* Wikipedia, s.v. "Congress of Vienna," accessed June 19, 2020, https://en.wikipedia.org/wiki/Congress_of_Vienna.

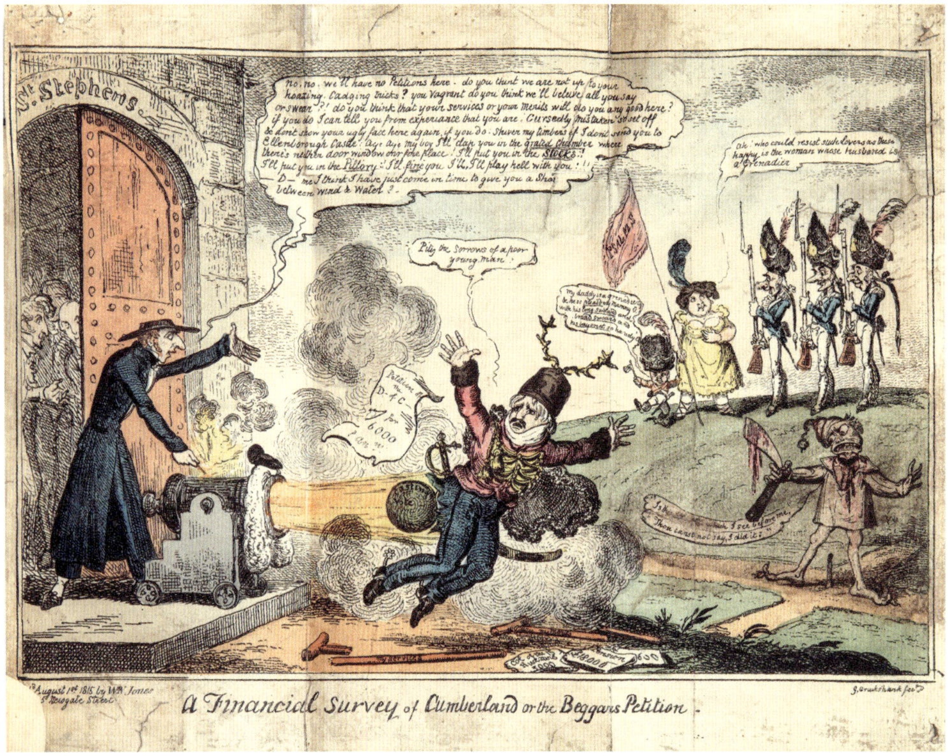

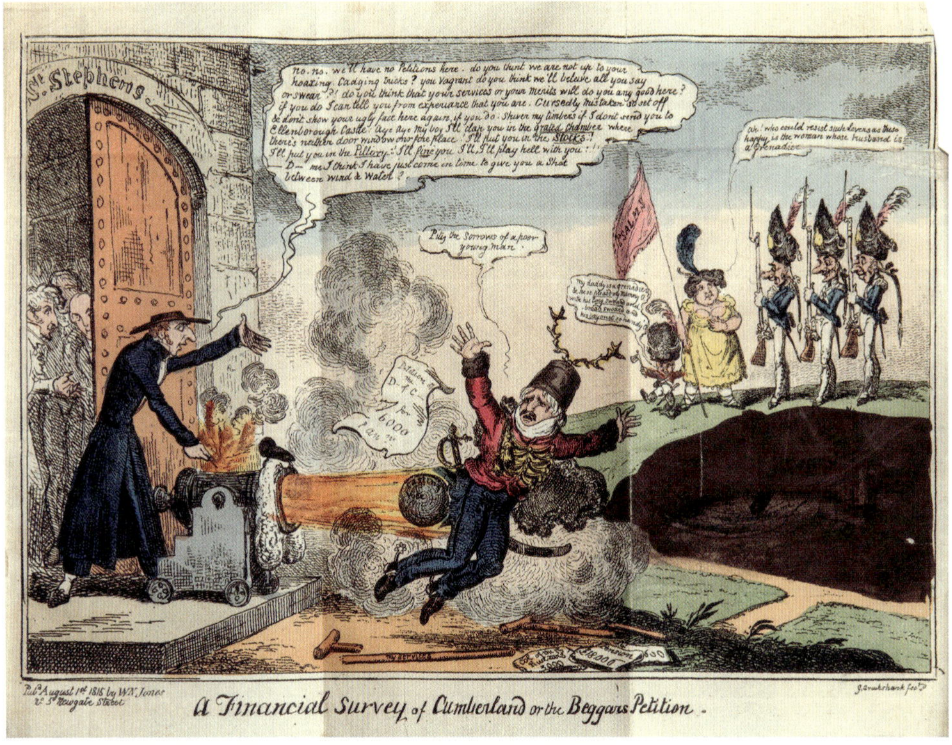

ITEM NOS. 14C & 14D. "Volume X: The Financial Survey of Cumberland or the Beggar's Petition." Pubd. August 1st, 1815 by WN Jones, No. 5 Newgate. G. Cruikshank fecit. BOTH CENSORED AND UNCENSORED PRINTS. Hand-colored etching depicting the Duke of Cumberland, Ernest Augustus (1771–1851), fifth son of George III, who became King of Hanover in 1837 at the death of his older brother, William IV. He married his German first cousin, a woman of questionable morals, the year before. The couple was barred from Court not only for the duchess's promiscuity, but also for the Duke's rumored history of murderous behavior. He is shown here (wearing the horned headgear of a cuckold) being expelled from Parliament by a cannonball fired by Lord Cochrane, whose single vote had defeated the bill that would have increased the Duke's annual stipend. The Duchess looks longingly at three grotesque Grenadiers, saying "Ah! Who could resist such Lovers as these." In the uncensored version, one sees to the lower right the weird small figure of the Duke's valet, dressed only in a nightshirt, who allegedly cut his own throat after unsuccessfully trying to murder the Duke in 1810. Popular rumor had it that the Duke had murdered him. BMS 12815.

15

"An Arch Design, Intended for: Boney's Triumphal Entry into Paris!!!" G Ck Pub, Jany 1812 by J. Johnson, 96 Cheapside. Hand-colored etching depicting an ironic Arc de Triomphe from which Liberty, suspended by the feet from a gallows, blows a trumpet welcoming Napoleon as he returns from his disastrous Russian campaign. BMS #1991, 0720.48.[68]

16

"Charioteer Snip on Rising Ground." Priscilla Groote, invt. G. Cruikshank, scupl. Hand-colored etching by George Cruikshank after a drawing by Priscilla Groote, an amateur. Published by Laurie & Whittle, London, 1813. Broadside minus verses making fun of a wealthy tailor driving his own carriage made with all the trimmings of his trade, with the wife inside and an ill-equipped footman on the pincushion behind. BMS #1865, 1111.2068.

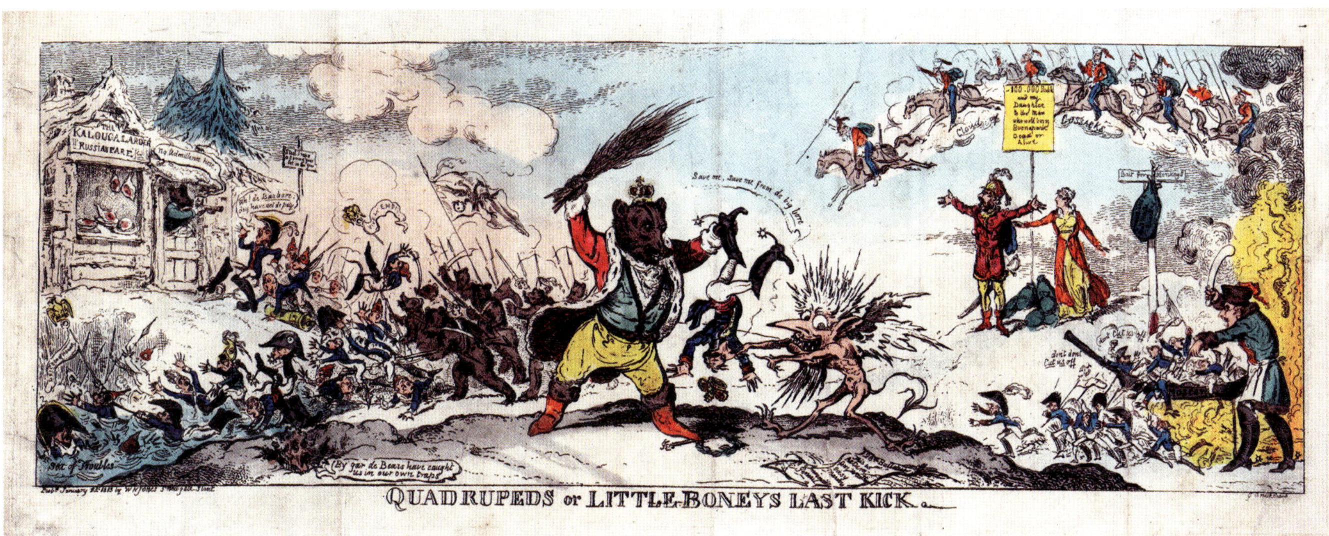

ITEM NO. 17

17

"Quadrupeds or Little Boney's Last Kick." Hand-colored etching, G. Cruikshank, Pub.d WN Jones, 1 Jany 1813. (Frontispiece foldout etching for *The Scourge*, Volume v, January 1, 1813.) A wonderful depiction of Napoleon's debacle at the hands of the Russian bear and Jack Frost after the burning of Moscow. BMS #1865, 1111.2062 (no image).

---

68. The Arc de Triomphe was commissioned in 1806 by Emperor Napoleon after his victory at Austerlitz, but not completed until 1836 during the reign of King Louis Phillippe. In 1810, Napoleon had a wooden mock-up of the completed arch built to celebrate his entry into Paris with his new wife, Archduchess Marie-Louise of Austria.

18

[Legend in Russian above image.] "Review of the French Troops on their Returning March through Smolensko – Altho their Dress is not gaudy it is warm & that is the principle thing!! Vide – the Hamburg Correspondenten for 1812 – No. 180 –14th March–" G. Cruikshank, Publ. May 27th, 1813 by H. Humphrey, St. James Street. This is one of several etchings Cruikshank designed using etchings created by Russian artists who were lampooning Napoleon as he retreated from Moscow. BMS 12718. See image on page 12.

19

"Hard Times or, O Dear What shall we do. O dear what shall become of us?!!" Pubd. Feb'y 10th 1814, by T. Tegg, Cheapside, London. It was customary in London for unemployed work-people to perambulate the streets with the tools of their trade, asking for alms. According to BMS 12185, hard times were produced by an unusually hard frost in February 1814. Surely, however, the long war with France was also straining British resources. Here, the procession is led by gardeners, next three grotesque apothecaries, followed by two artists, the more prominent being Cruikshank himself, thin and knock-kneed, holding a pole to which are tied palette, portfolio, brushes, and a large document: "Mr West's Speech on the Gloomy State of the Arts." At his feet, a paper inscribed "Poor Shanks fect" serves as signature to the print. His companion is believed to be Benjamin West, wearing spectacles and a broad-brimmed hat.[69] They are followed by two melancholy poets; next Napoleon with a rope round his neck dragged by a demon carrying a pole with an eagle on which is seated his baby son, the King of Rome. Four prostitutes follow, ending with the undertakers flourishing papers inscribed "Bill of Mortality" (the weekly list of deaths in London). BMS 12754.

ITEM NO. 19

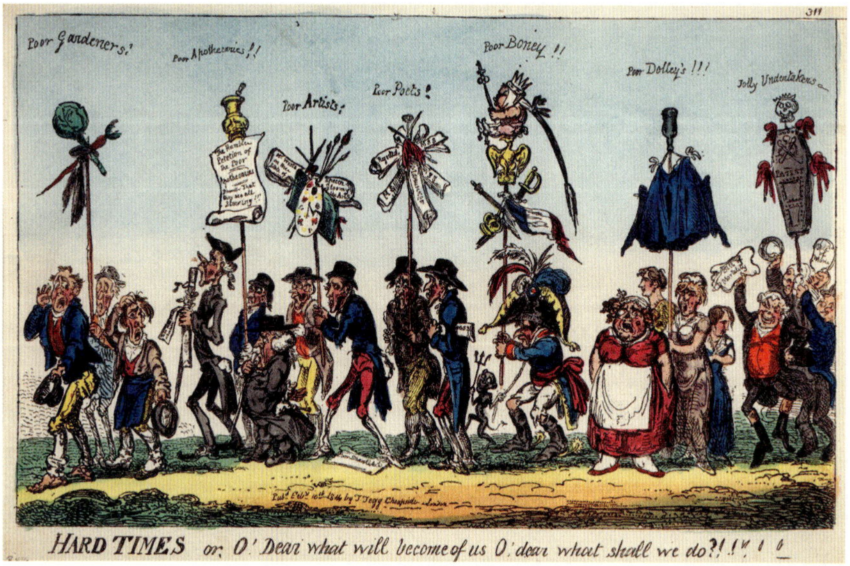

69. Benjamin West (1738–1820) was an American-born artist who painted famous historical scenes. Self-taught (like Cruikshank), West settled in London, gained valuable patronage, including King George III, and was largely responsible for launching the Royal Academy, of which he became the second president, after Sir Joshua Reynolds. Wikipedia, s.v. "Benjamin West," accessed June 13, 2020, https://en.wikipedia.org/wiki/Benjamin_West.

20

"The Affectionate Farewell or Kick for Kick." Hand-colored etching, London, R. Ackermann, 17 April, 1814. Unsigned. Thomas Rowlandson. BMS 8129.

21

"Complements & Congees or Little Boney's Surrender to the Tars of Old England." Publ. July 24, 1815, G. Cruikshank fecit. np. BM copy: After "1815" in the inscription, "by J Johnston Cheapside" added in pen to one impression. Cohn 1009.

22

"A Review of the New Grand Army. Capt. of Starved Banditty from the Alps. Ad Camp, The Aghast Emperor & His Two Friends & Pillars of the State, Butcher from Elba, Generalissimo from the Alps. Force, Meat balls for the Lads in Paris." BMS 8198: by William Heath (1795–1840); May 1815.

23

The Life of Napoleon, a Hudibrastic Poem in Fifteen Cantos. by Doctor Syntax [William Combe], embellished with Thirty Engravings by G. Cruikshank. London. Printed for T. Tegg, 111 Cheapside, Wm Allason, 31. New Bond Street & J. Dick, Edinburgh. 1815.

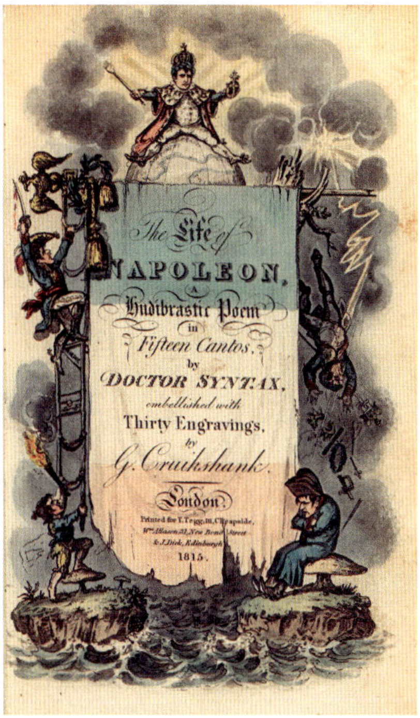

ITEM NO. 23

24

"Bank Restriction Note," published by William Hone, Jany 1819. Broadside, published and sold with "Bank Restriction Barometer." Britain replaced gold with paper currency in 1797. Bank notes were issued in small denominations and easily forged. To pass a forged 1£ note, innocently or not, resulted in the death penalty. Cruikshank claimed to have etched this design after walking past the gibbet opposite Newgate Prison with two women among the executed, and learning that they had each been executed for passing a forged 1£ note. The Note and Barometer were enormously popular. Cruikshank believed they were partially responsible for the reforms of the currency and of the death penalty that were to follow.[70] Note: This item is from the Zukor Album, Item No. 33 below on p. 55.

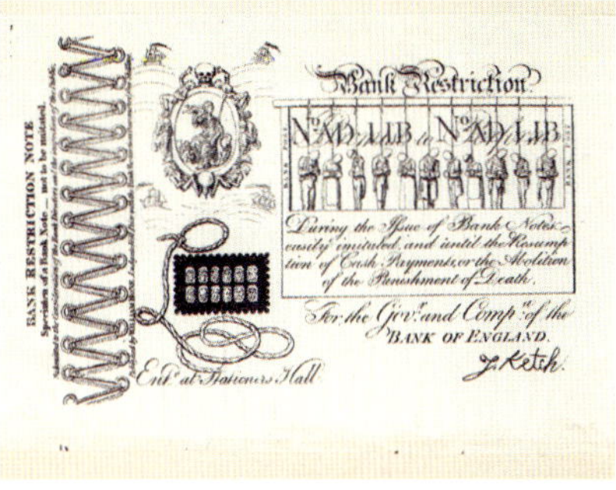

ITEM NO. 24

70. Patten, *George Cruikshank's Life,* 1:145–147.

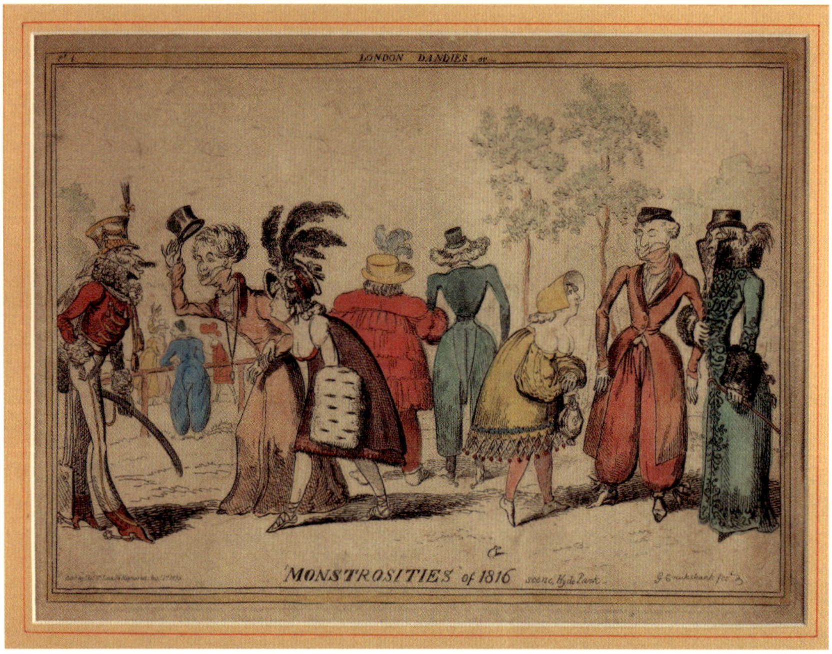

ITEM NO. 25. "Monstrosities of 1816 – Scene, Hyde Park." Compare with Leech's *Fashions of 1844*, Item No. 72.

25

"Monstrosities of 1816 – Scene, Hyde Park; Monstrosities of 1817; Monstrosities of 1819 & 1820." Set of three hand-colored etchings matted and framed with decorative orange and yellow bands surrounding each print. 1816 plate labeled at top: "Pl. 1 London Dandies"; all three at bottom: "Publ. by Thos. McLean, 26 Haymarket, Aug. 1, 1835. G. Cruikshank fecit." Second issue. First published by George Humphrey in 1816, 1817, and 1820.

26

Political Tracts. Six unnumbered volumes containing 42 pamphlets written by William Hone, illustrated with numerous wood engravings by George Cruikshank, published 1819–1821. Each volume has five to ten separate tracts, including "John Bull's Constitutional Apple Pie," "Frown from the Crown," "The Political House that Jack Built," and "The Political Queen that Jack Loves," most of which were printed by Hone himself, a few by John Fairburn. Many of the pamphlets are of a much later edition (e.g., Twelfth or Seventh), but all are dated as being printed in the year first published or a year thereafter, demonstrating the enormity of their immediate success.

26A

The Queen's Matrimonial Ladder. A National Toy, with Fourteen Step Scenes; and Illustrations in Verse, with Eighteen Other Cuts. By the Author of "The Political House that Jack Built." Sixth Edition. London: Printed by and for William Hone, Ludgate-Hill. 1820. This pamphlet and The Toy together, One Shilling,[71] TOGETHER WITH THE TOY

71. Cohn mistakenly dates this pamphlet as 1826. Cohn, *George Cruikshank, A Catalogue Raisonné,* 680.

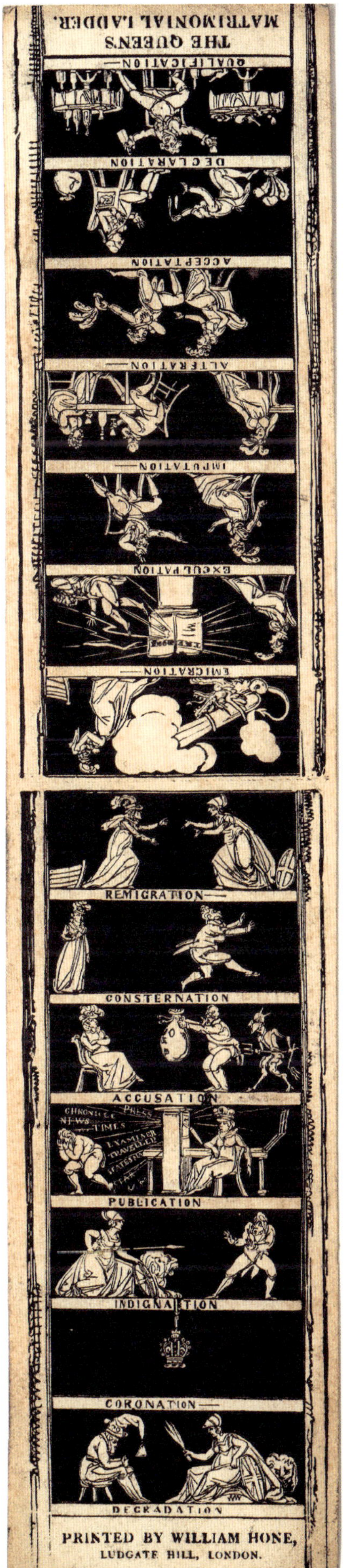

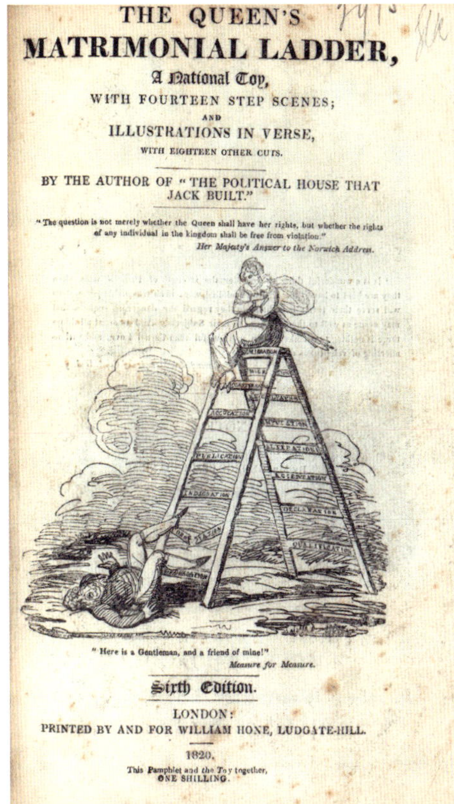

THE QUEEN'S
MATRIMONIAL LADDER,
A National Toy,
WITH FOURTEEN STEP SCENES;
AND
ILLUSTRATIONS IN VERSE,
WITH EIGHTEEN OTHER CUTS.

BY THE AUTHOR OF "THE POLITICAL HOUSE THAT JACK BUILT."

"The question is not merely whether the Queen shall have her rights, but whether the rights of any individual in the kingdom shall be free from violation."
Her Majesty's Answer to the Norwich Address.

" Here is a Gentleman, and a friend of mine!"
Measure for Measure.

Sixth Edition.

LONDON:
PRINTED BY AND FOR WILLIAM HONE, LUDGATE-HILL.
1820.
This Pamphlet and the Toy together,
ONE SHILLING.

ITEM NO. 26A. Title page and Toy Matrimonial Ladder. A narrow pasteboard strip, which folds in the middle, with 14 tiny wood engravings by Cruikshank (done in Bewick's "white-line" style, white lines carved out of the printed black background), adapted from the 14 steps illustrated in the pamphlet.

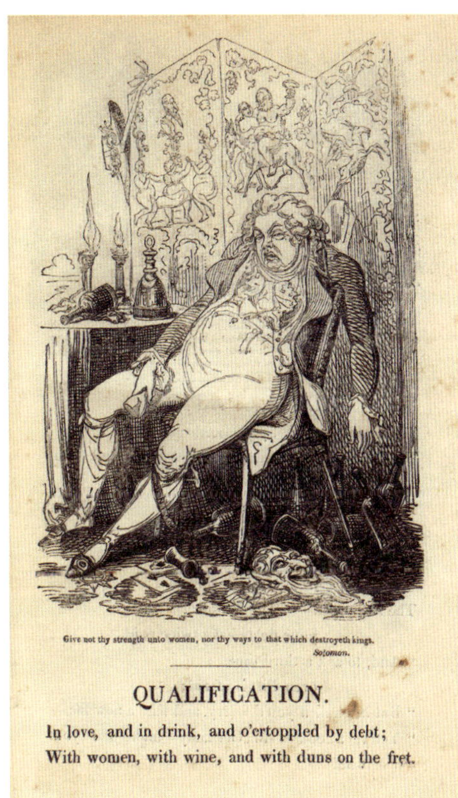

Give not thy strength unto women, nor thy ways to that which destroyeth kings.
Solomon.

QUALIFICATION.

In love, and in drink, and o'ertoppled by debt;
With women, with wine, and with duns on the fret.

ITEM NO. 26A. "Qualification." This woodcut illustrates the first of the 14 steps of the matrimonial ladder. The Prince of Wales married his cousin, Princess Caroline, in 1795, only because his father, King George III, had refused to bail him out of his staggering debts resulting from his dissolute lifestyle unless he did so. The final step is "Degradation." The degree of degradation with which Cruikshank graphically depicts the Prince (now George IV) was a tribute to Britain's mild censorship at the time.

CARDBOARD LADDER IN ITS ORIGINAL ENVELOPE. The two-sided ladder was a familiar device used by Cruikshank to show the rise and fall of princes. See, e.g., frontispiece for *The Life of Napoleon, a Hudibrastic Poem in Fifteen Cantos* (Item No. 18). Here it is used to illustrate the rise and fall of a marriage to the dissolute Prince (who had become King six months earlier), and to defend Princess Caroline of Brunswick in her fight against her husband's efforts to divorce her so as to prevent her from becoming Queen. Technically, the King was unsuccessful in proceeding with the divorce, but prevented her from attending his coronation on July 19, 1821, and she died three weeks later. Many radicals warmed to Caroline's defense mainly because of the Prince's unpopularity and dissipation.

26B

The Divine Right of Kings to Govern Wrong. Dedicated to the Holy Alliance. Fourth Edition. London: Printed for William Hone, 45 Ludgate-Hill. 1821. One Shilling. Illustrated with two striking woodcuts by George Cruikshank. According to the Hone Archives, *The Divine Right of Kings to Govern Wrong* is Hone's heavily edited and partially rewritten version of Daniel Defoe's *Jure Divino* (1706), attacking the concept of the divine right of kings, published in reaction to two contemporary historical events. The "Holy Alliance" was organized by Francis I of Austria, Tsar Alexander I of Russia, and King Frederick William III of Prussia after the defeat of Napoleon in 1815 to establish the concept that Christian morality was the only legitimate principle upon which to rule. The Alliance was soon joined by the newly restored Louis XVIII of France and the British Prince Regent. For the radicals in Europe, the emergence of the Holy Alliance signaled a shoring up of the powers of the Church and the monarchies against the will of "the People." In Britain, the religious and

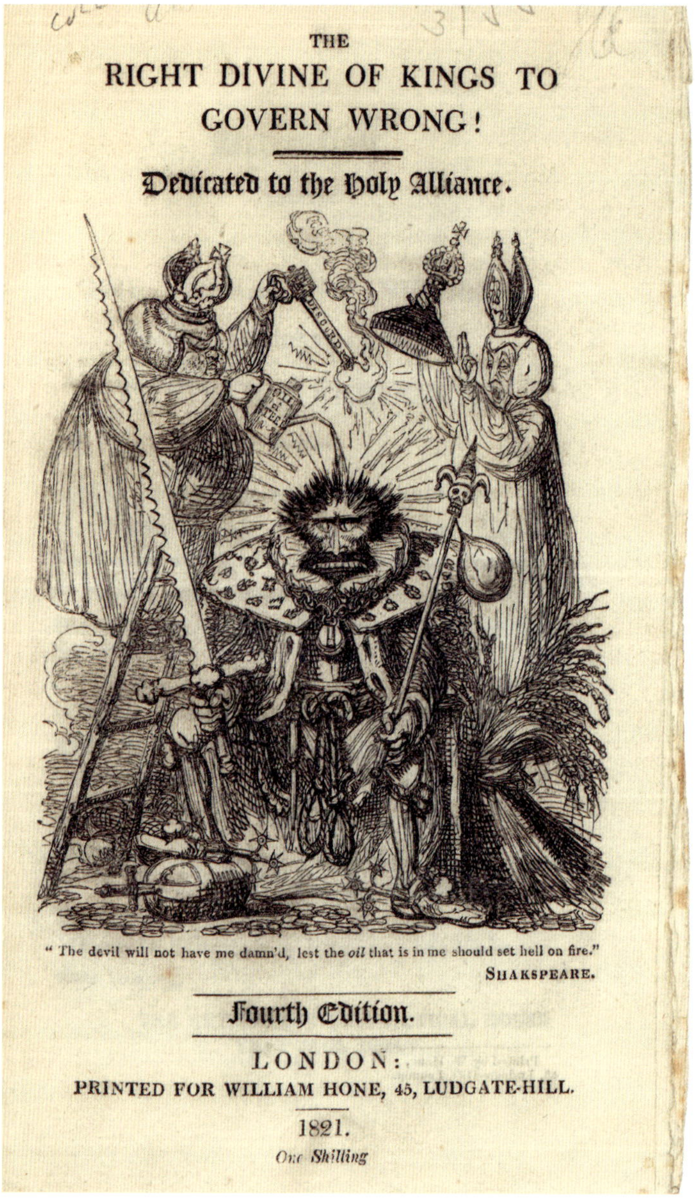

THE
RIGHT DIVINE OF KINGS TO
GOVERN WRONG!

Dedicated to the Holy Alliance.

"The devil will not have me damn'd, lest the *oil* that is in me should set hell on fire."
SHAKSPEARE.

Fourth Edition.

LONDON:
PRINTED FOR WILLIAM HONE, 45, LUDGATE-HILL.
1821.
One Shilling

ITEM NO. 26B. Cover.

moral goals of the Alliance further exposed the hypocrisy of the Prince Regent and confirmed the radicals' suspicions of a corrupt collusion between church and state to suppress emerging democratic ideals. The second event, the "Queen Caroline Affair" (where the King had arguably used extralegal methods and the clergy to rid himself of his consort), energized journalists and satirists like Hone to bring this long-simmering ideological clash (the rights of the monarch vs. the laws adhered to by the rest of society) into prominence.[72]

27

"A Late Arrival At Mother Wood's." Pub.d June 19, 1820, by G. Humphrey, 27 St. James Street. Hand-colored etching attributed to I. Robert Cruikshank. [British] National Portrait Gallery #D17921.

28

"The Genius of History, or Dressing for a Mask'd Ball at Naples." Pubd October 1820, by G. Humphrey, 27 St. James St., signed at bottom of print "Selim sc." Hand-colored etching. The Princess of Wales, preening before a large glass above a console table, with Bergami holding a scarf and a box of "Essence Bergamy" wearing orders. One can see Vesuvius through the window. This print has been attributed to Theodore Lane, who often used the pseudonym Selim. (See the print collection housed at the Lewis Walpole Library in Farmington, Connecticut.)[73]

---

72. The William Hone BioText, a biography, bibliography, and etext archive, edited by Kyle Grimes, https://honearchive.org/etexts/right-divine/right-divine-home.html.

73. Yale University Library Catalogue entry, http://hdl.handle.net/10079/bibid/13850418. Theodore Lane (1800–1828) was a talented young satirist who died at age 28 in a tragic accident. While waiting for a friend at the horse repository in Gray's Inn Road, he stepped on a skylight and fell to the pavement below. Wikipedia, s.v. "Theodore Lane," accessed June 19, 2020, https://en.wikipedia.org/wiki/Theodore_Lane.

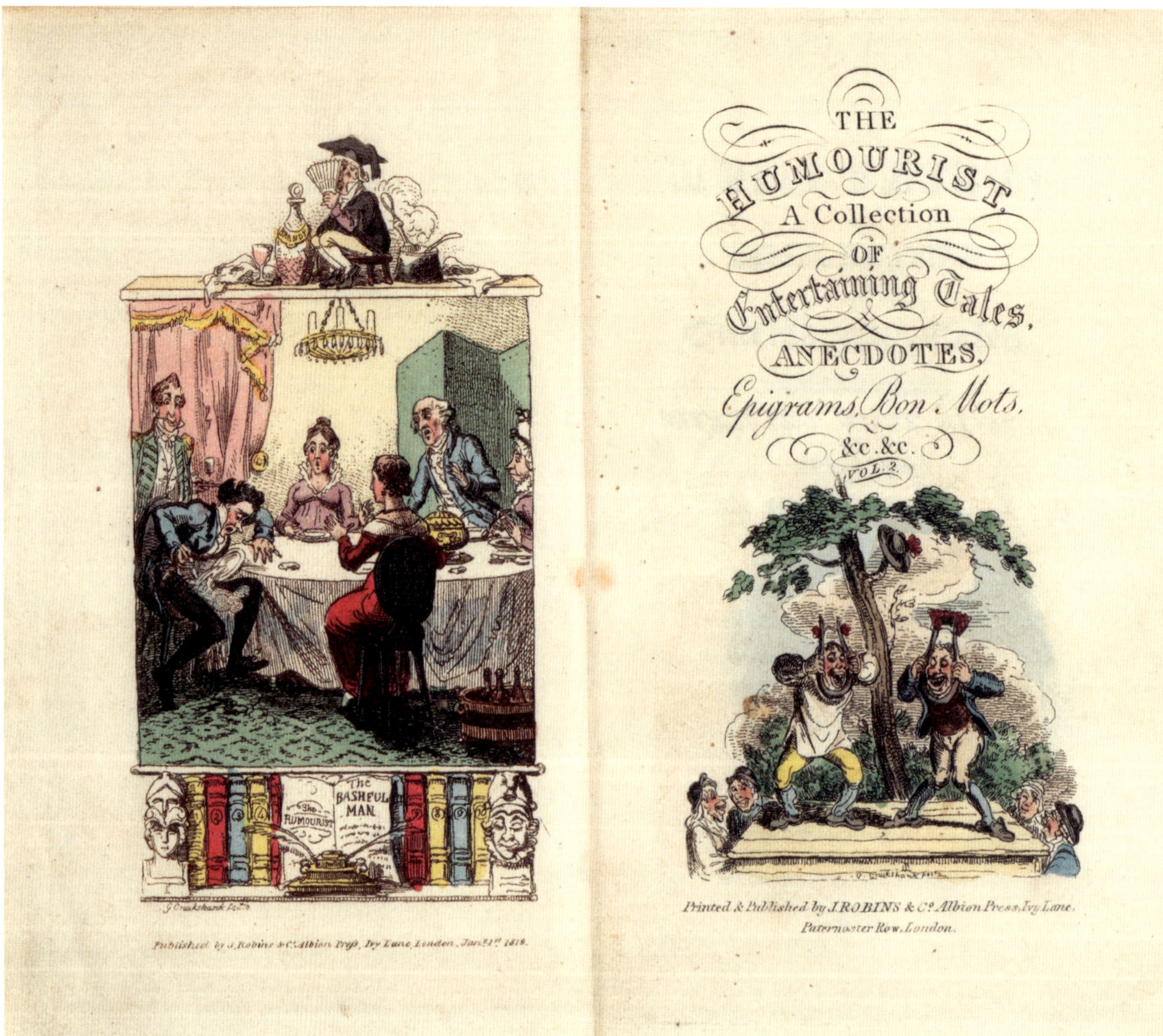

ITEM NO. 29. Frontispiece and engraved title page to Volume 2.

29

The Humourist: A Collection of Entertaining Tales, Anecdotes, Repartees, Witty Sayings, Epigrams, Bon Mots, Jeu d'Esprits, &c. Carefully Selected. London: Printed and Published by J. Robins and Co., Albion Press, Ivy-Lane, Paternoster-Row, 1819. Four volumes. It is thought that Robins issued 40 six-penny parts, each stitched into green wrappers with a colored etching in each, during 1819 and 1820. See Cohn 419. This is the first book edition in their original pink paper printed boards with Cruikshank's design engraved on the covers and 40 hand-colored etchings. As per Cohn 419, Volume 1 is not so designated on its title page, which bears the date 1819; Volumes 2, 3, and 4 are dated respectively 1819, 1819, and 1820.

30

Lessons of Thrift, Published for General Benefit, by a Member of the Save-All Club. London: Printed for Thomas Boys of Ludgate Hill. 1820. Written by John Wilson Roy Crawford; with 12 hand-colored etchings designed and etched by I.R. Cruikshank.

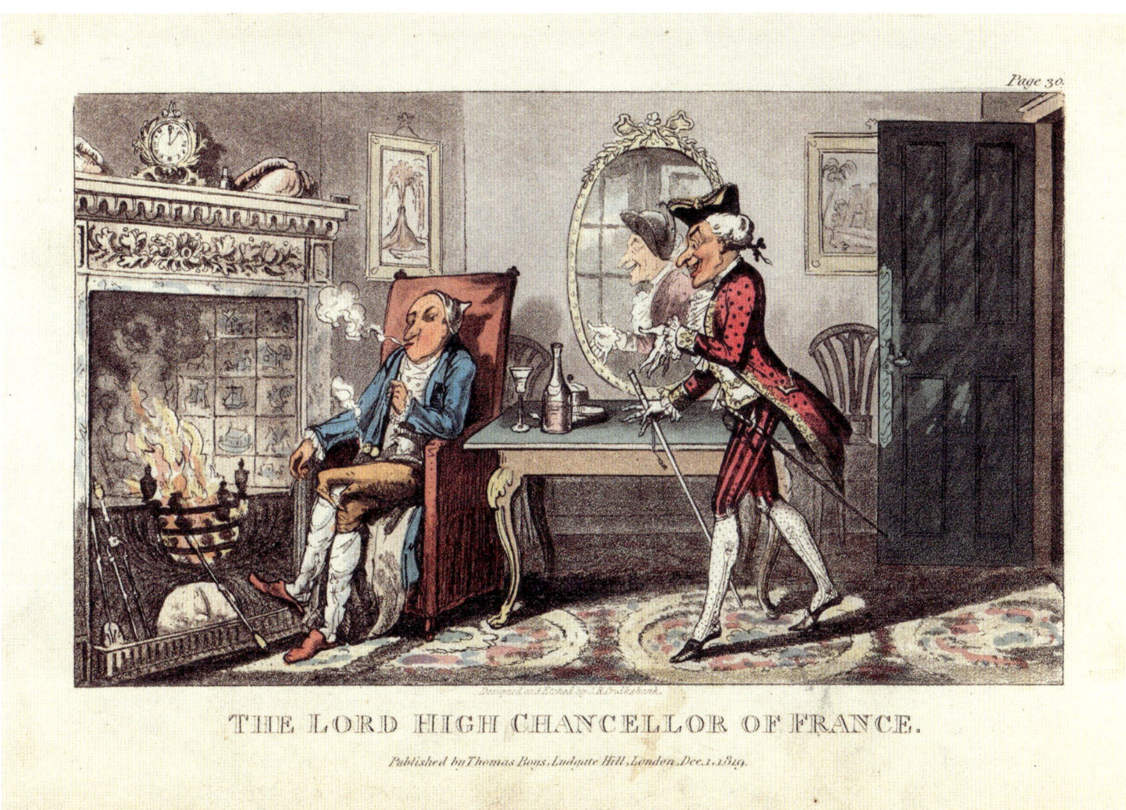

ITEM NO. 30. Plate at page 30: "The Lord High Chancellor of France," Publ. by Thomas Boys, of Ludgate Hill, London, Dec. 3, 1819.

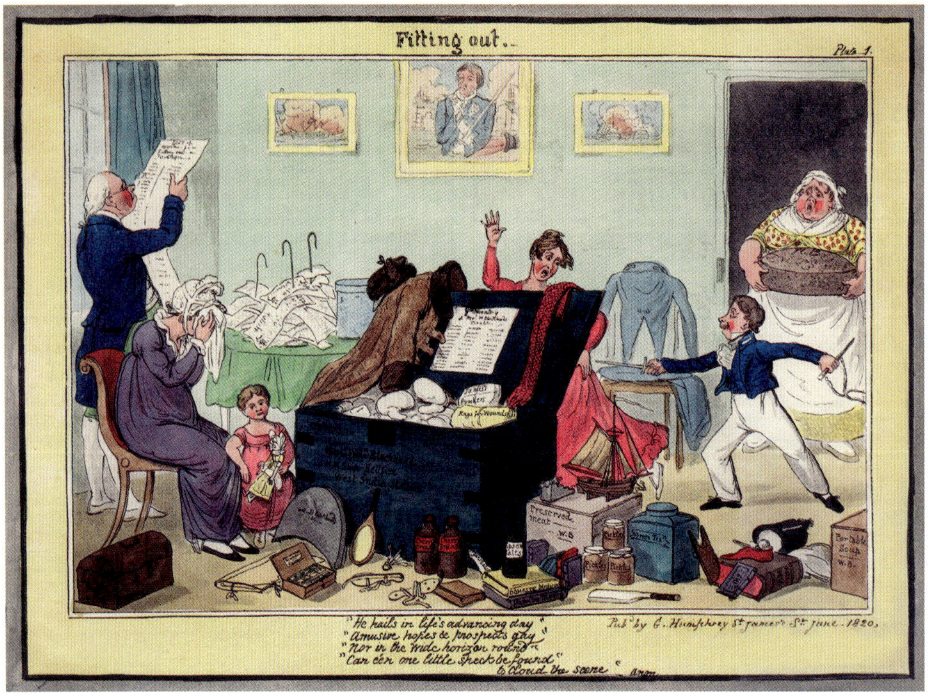

ITEM NO. 31. Plate 1. "Fitting Out." First state (1820).

31

The Progress of a Midshipman, Exemplified in the Career of Master Blockhead: In Eight Coloured Prints Designed by a Naval Officer, and Engraved by G. Cruikshank. London. Published by G. Humphrey, 27, St. James's Street. 1821. Album containing eight hand-colored etchings by Cruikshank after eight drawings by Frederick Marryat, each dated 1820 and bearing Marryat's anchor mark and Cruikshank's signature as sculpt. First edition, first state. Together with the same eight plates by Cruikshank after Marryat with same anchor mark, hand-colored with much darker and less delicate coloring, each dated 1821. First edition, second state, together with the original wrapper for the 1821 series and an early undated but lettered proof of Plate 1, "Fitting Out." Cohn 1874. Captain Frederick Marryat (1792–1848) was a British Royal Navy officer, novelist, and a good friend and collaborator of Cruikshank's. He is noted today as an early pioneer of the sea story, and for a system of maritime signaling known as Marryat's Code.

32

Life in London; or, the Day and Night Scenes of Jerry Hawthorn, Esq. and his elegant friend Corinthian Tom, accompanied by Bob Logic, the Oxonian, in their Rambles and Sprees through the Metropolis. By Pierce Egan. Embellished with Thirty-Six scenes from Real Life, designed and etched by I. R. & G. Cruikshank; and enriched also with numerous original Designs on wood, by the same Artists. London: Printed for Sherwood, Neely, and Jones, Paternoster-Row. 1821. First issue of first book edition. Cohn 262. First published in 12 monthly parts from October 1820 through July 1821. This copy has a single, heavy leaf with a hand-colored stipple-engraved portrait of George Cruikshank, signed in pencil "GCk as designer and FWP [Frederick W. Pailthorpe] as scupl.," and what appears to be an original sepia pen drawing below it, signed "Rob't Cruikshank 1828," bound in, facing the list of illustrations on p. xv. The production of the illustrations for *Life in London* was a true collaboration between the brothers. Each etching states, "Drawn & Engraved by I.R. & G. Cruikshank," except for the frontispiece, which has no designation of designer or engraver.

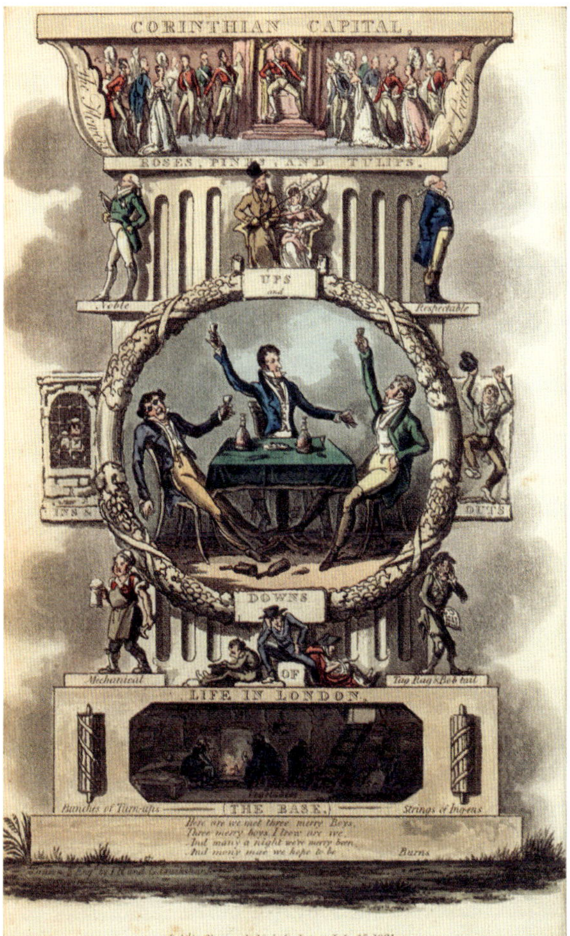

ITEM NO. 32A. Frontispiece.

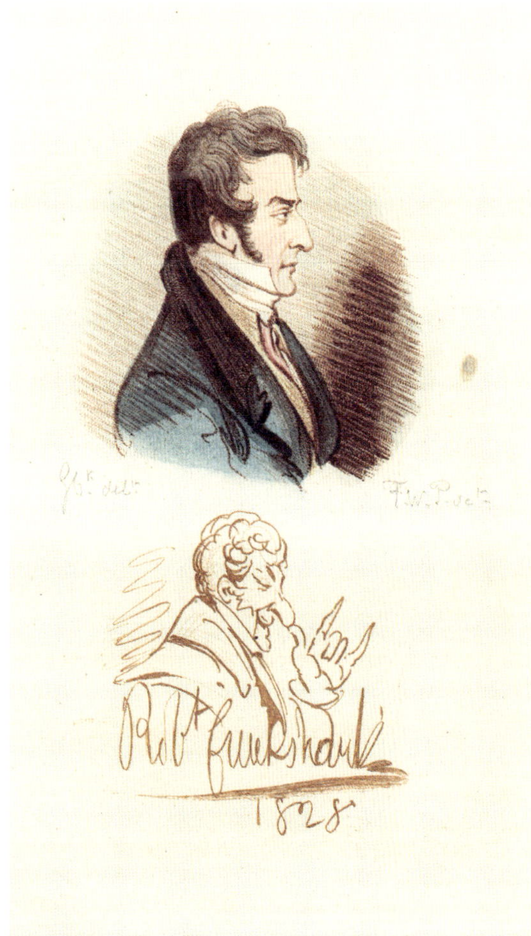

ITEM NO. 32B. Leaf with the two brothers' self-portraits.

33

Original Drawings by Isaac, Robert and George Cruikshank. Collector's Album. *Ex Libris* Adolph Zukor. A large album filled with original drawings and watercolor studies on paper for many of George Cruikshank's published works, plus a number of sketches never published, and several of Robert's drawings as well. Adolph Zukor (1873–1976) was an Austro-Hungarian-born American film producer best known as one of the three founders of Paramount Pictures. This is a treasure trove of original sketches by GCk, although many of the works are detached from their mounts.

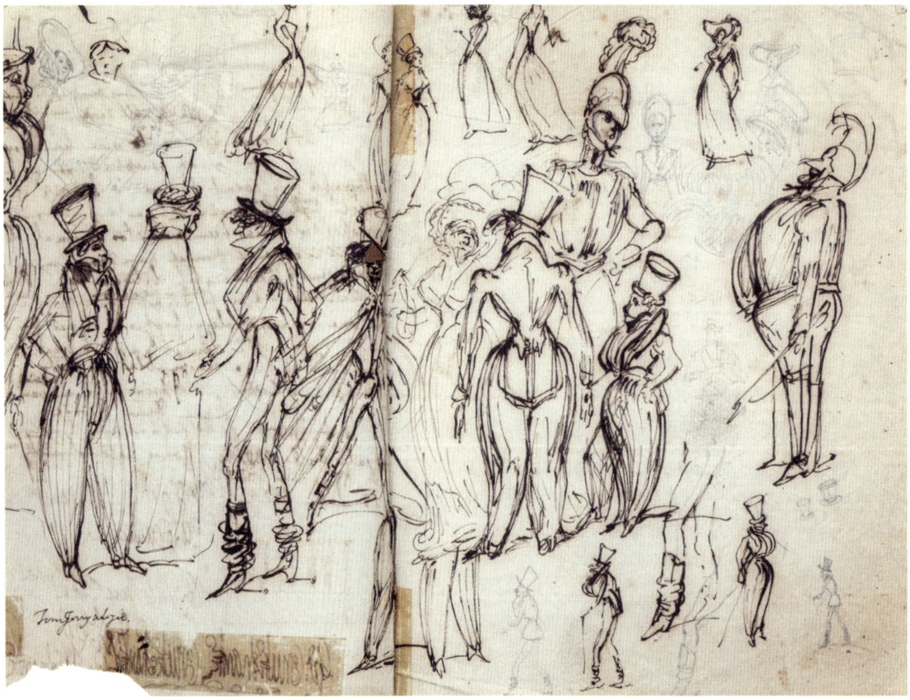

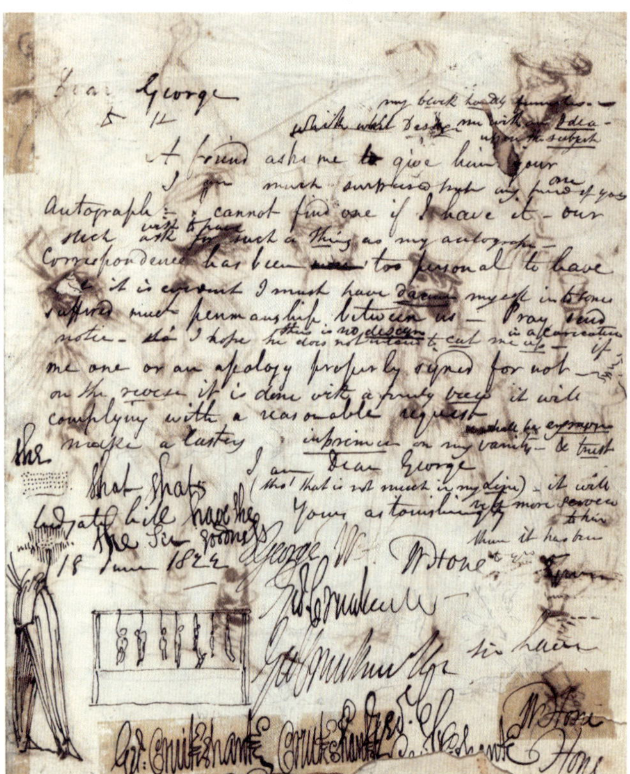

ITEM NOS. 33A & 33B. Autograph letter in sepia ink, dated 18 June, 1822, from William Hone to GCk,* asking him for an autograph for a friend, saying their correspondence had been too personal to be sent. The letter is written with much familiar jocularity indicating their long and warm personal and professional relationship. As with many a drawing sketched by or letter received by Cruikshank, every blank space is covered with additional sketches and doodles. Here, he writes his large signature several times at the bottom of Hone's letter, and seems to mimic Hone's signature as well. In addition, he draws the gibbet used on the "Bank Restriction Note" (see Item No. 24). ON THE INSIDE DOUBLE FOLD OF THE LETTER are numerous ink sketches of dandies with an ink inscription: "TomJerry & Logic," characters he had just been sketching for *Life in London.*

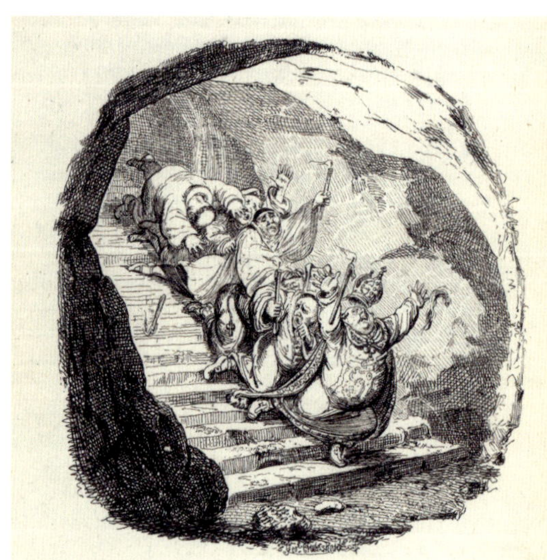

ITEM NO. 37. Illustration for "The Downfall of the Holy Church," Part I, Point IX, p. 42.

* A penciled note at the bottom of the mat on which this letter is pasted indicates that it was acquired from Rosenbach on June 9, 1923.

33c.

Autograph letter, dated Ivy Lane, 24 Dec. 1827, from James Robins [GCk's publisher] to GCk advising him that he hadn't heard from Clement [William Inell Clement, owner of *Bell's Life in London*] and thus was compelled to "give him notice of action." Cruikshank's note on the back refers to "Mr. Clement, the proprietor of Bell's Blackguard[?] Life in London," and complains that he is "using such large quantities of that valuable [illegible]"[74]

34

Life in Paris; comprising the Rambles, Sprees, and Amours of Dick Wildfire, of Corinthian Celebrity and his Bang-up Companion, Squire Jenkins and Captain O'Shuffleton; with the Whimsical Adventures of the Halibut Family; Including Sketches of a Variety of other Eccentric Characters in the French Metropolis. By David Carey. Embellished with Twenty-One Coloured Plates, representing Scenes from Real Life, designed and engraved by Mr. George Cruikshank. Enriched also with Twenty-two Engravings on Wood, drawn by the same Artist, and executed by Mr. White. London: Printed for John Fairburn, Broadway, Ludgate-Hill; Sold by Sherwood, Neely and Jones; Longman, 1822.

35

Eccentric Tales from the German of W. F. von Kosewitz with Illustrations by George Cruikshank from sketches by Alfred Crowquill. London: James Robins and Co. Ivy Lane, Paternoster Row. MDCCCXXVII. Twenty hand-colored etchings. First book edition. First published in four parts with five etchings per part. Charming illustrations.

36

Pearce Egan's Finish to the Adventures of Tom, Jerry, and Logic, in their pursuits through Life in and out of London: Illustrated by the pencil of Mr. Robert Cruikshank, in 36 Scenes from Real Life, & enriched with several Designs on Wood by the same Artist. Dedicated to His Most Gracious Majesty King George the Fourth. London: Printed by C. Baynes, 13, Duke-street, Lincoln's-inn-fields, for G. Virtue, 26, Ivy Lane, Paternoster Row; Bath Street, Bristol; and Great Ancoates Street, Manchester. 1830.

37

Points of Humour. Illustrated by the designs of George Cruikshank. London: Published by C. Baldwyn, Newgate Street. Parts I and II. 1823, 1824. With ten etchings and eight woodcuts.

---

74. See Patten, *George Cruikshank's Life,* 1:300, 301, for an account of the dispute between GCk and Bell's over the pirating of his work.

38

German Popular Stories. Translated from the Kinder und HausMarchen. Collected by M. M. Grimm from Oral Tradition. Published by Charles Baldwyn, London, 1824. Second English Edition. Vol. II. Published by James Robins & Co., London, 1826. First English Edition. Twelve etchings in Vol. I; ten etchings in Vol. II. These volumes were the first English translations of the original tales written by the Grimm brothers. Jacob Ludwig Karl Grimm (1785–1863) and Wilhelm Carl Grimm (1786–1859) were German academics, philologists, lexicographers, and authors who together collected and published folklore. Their classic collection, *Children's and Household Tales (Kinder-und Hausmärchen),* was published in two volumes – the first in 1812, the second in 1815. Between the first editions of 1812/1815 and the seventh (and final) edition of the combined tales in 1857, they revised their collection many times, so that it grew from 156 stories to more than 200.[75] Baldwyn learned about the tales from a family member of his printer, Edgar Taylor, who had just returned from studying in Gottingen where he had enjoyed reading the newly published stories, and offered to translate them for Baldwyn.[76] Cruikshank's wee copper etchings of the Grimms' elves and ogres, some of the best he ever did, met with great applause and were a foundation of his reputation as one of the finest etchers of all time.[77]

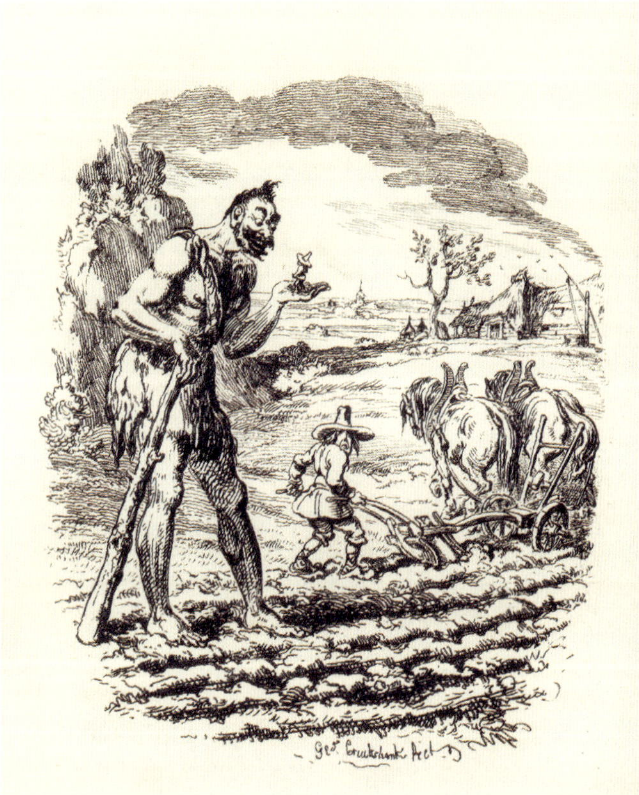

ITEM NO. 38B. Volume II: Illustration for "The Young Giant and the Tailor."

ITEM NO. 38A. Volume I: Illustration for "The Elves and the Shoemaker." See image on page 10.

---

75. Wikipedia, s.v. "Brothers Grimm," accessed June 13, 2020, https://en.wikipedia.org/wiki/Brothers_Grimm.
76. Patten, *George Cruikshank's Life,* 1:240.
77. In 1863, John Ruskin (1819–1900), the leading English art critic of the Victorian era, was so taken with the original Grimms' tales and Cruikshank's etchings that he asked for them to be republished and wrote an introduction to the new edition. Of the illustrations, he writes in the Preface (xiii), "They are of quite sterling and admirable art, in a class precisely in elevation to the character of the tales which they illustrate; and the original etchings…were unrivalled in masterfulness since Rembrandt; (in some qualities of delineation unrivalled even by him.)" *German Popular Stories.* With Illustrations after the original designs of George Cruikshank. Edited by Edgar Taylor, with Introduction by John Ruskin, M.A., London: John Camden Hotten, Piccadilly. [1863].

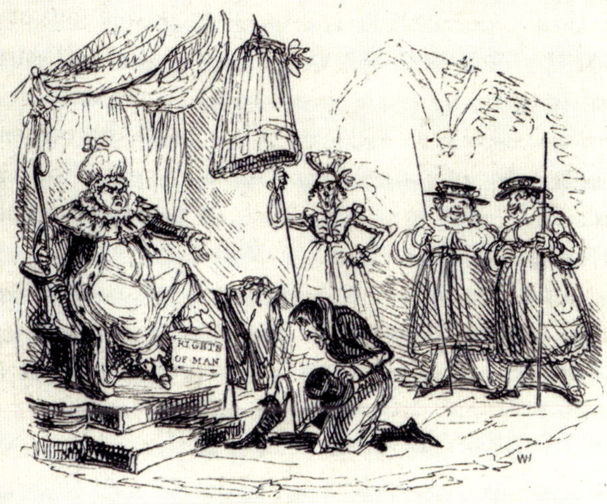

Petticoat Government.

p. 146.

ITEM NO. 39. Vignette illustrating "A White Sergeant, or the Petticoat Government." A sketch of poor Mr. H., "a very respectable law-stationer," who resisted the dictates of Mrs. H., and as a result, suffered much in the hands of the law.

39

Mornings at Bow Street; A Selection of the Most Humorous and Entertaining Reports Which Have Appeared in the Morning Herald. By Mr. Wight (Bow Street Reporter to the Morning Herald). With Twenty-One Illustrative Drawings By George Cruikshank. London: Printed for Charles Baldwyn, Newgate Street. MDCCCXXIV. All illustrations are woodcut vignettes, each on a separate page. By the mid-18th century, Bow Street, near Covent Garden, was known for where everyday crimes and petty disputes met the law. In 1750, Henry Fielding had established the Bow Street Runners, an early voluntary police force. From 1832 on, the Metropolitan Police operated a station house on the street; and the Bow Street Magistrates' Court was constructed there in 1879.[78] *Mornings at Bow Street*, like *Points of Humour*, was a precursor to a burgeoning new journalistic genre, the sketch, here humorous pieces from the *Morning Herald* written by John Wight, based on court testimony depicting "a few eccentric characters or a momentary incident, to capture something of the fleeting quality of urban experience."[79] The most celebrated example of this genre was *Sketches by Boz,* written 12 years later by another young journalist, Charles Dickens.

40

Peter Schlemihl. From the German of Lamotte Fouque. With Plates by George Cruikshank. London: G and W. B. Whittaker, Ave Maria Lane. 1824.

---

78. Wikipedia, s.v. "Bow Street," accessed on June 20, 2020, https://en.wikipedia.org/wiki/Bow Street.
79. Patten, *George Cruikshank's Life,* 1:281.

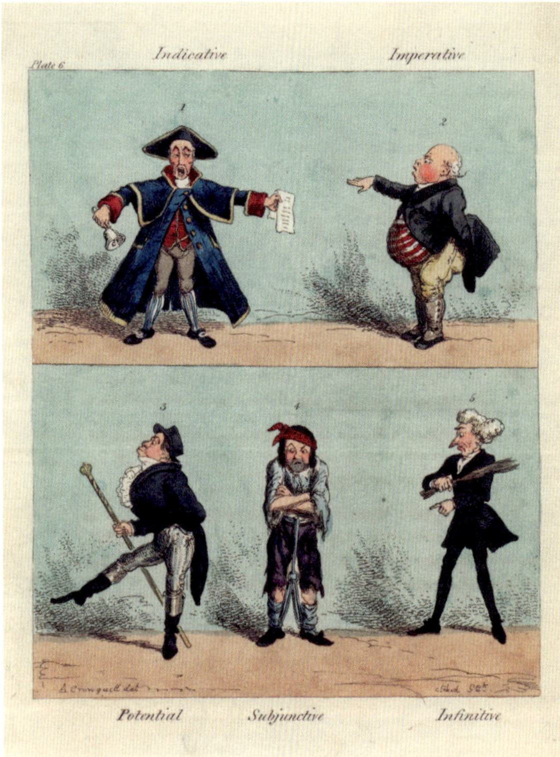

ITEM NO. 41. Plate 6.

41

The Holiday Grammar. By Alfred Crowquill, Esq. Etched by George Cruikshanks [*sic*], For the Present Generation, Passing Murray, Dilworth, and All Past Grammarians in Simplicity, And As fitting for the future as the present Generation; Wherein Each Article is Hieroglyphically and Laconically Defined, and Adapted to the Capacity of All Degrees, whether Positive, Comparative, or Superlative. London: Printed for S. Knights, Sweetings-Alley, Royal-Exchange. 1825. Six hand-colored numbered plates each labeled "A Crowquill del." and "Etched by G.Ck."

42

Greenwich Hospital, a Series of Naval Sketches, descriptive of the Life of a Man-Of-War's Man. By an Old Sailor [Matthew Henry Barker], with Illustrations by George Cruikshank. London: Published by James Robins and Co. Ivy lane, Paternoster Row; and Joseph Robins, Jun. and Co. Lower Ormond Quay, Dublin. MDCCCXXVI. First book edition. Originally published in four parts with 12 hand-colored etchings and 16 woodcuts in the text.

43

Album with four series of etchings, each with an uncolored wrapper and six plates with numerous vignettes on each. The little scenes in these pages are very fine. It is almost impossible to choose the few to be shown in this catalogue and, of course, will be far harder to pick which plate will be put on exhibition. One needs the time and inclination to sit quietly, with good light and a loupe, to give proper attention to the wit and draftsmanship found in this album.

43A.

Illustrations of Time, Published May 1, 1827, by the Artist, 22 Myddelton Terrace, Pentonville. Sold by J. Robins & Co., Ivy Lane, Paternoster Row. Uncolored wrapper; six hand-colored and numbered plates each with inscription "Designed Etched and Published by George Cruikshank – May 1st 1827 –"

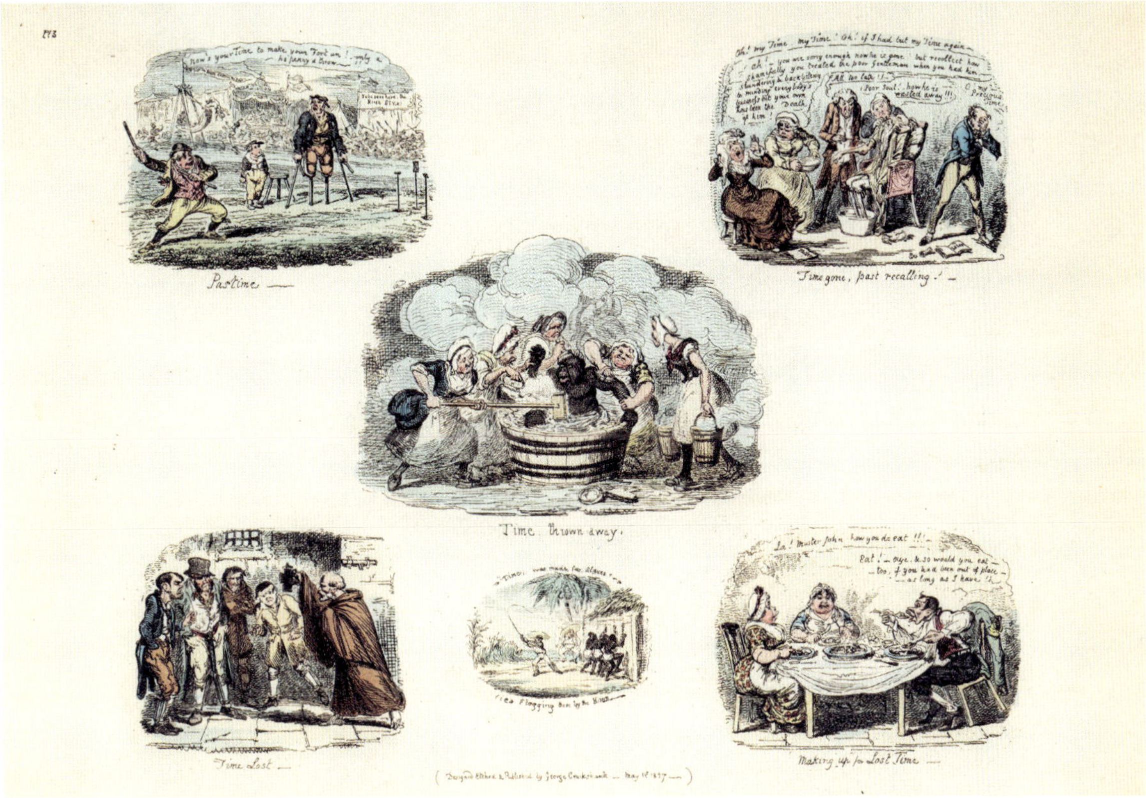

ITEM NO. 43A. Plate 3. "Time Thrown Away."

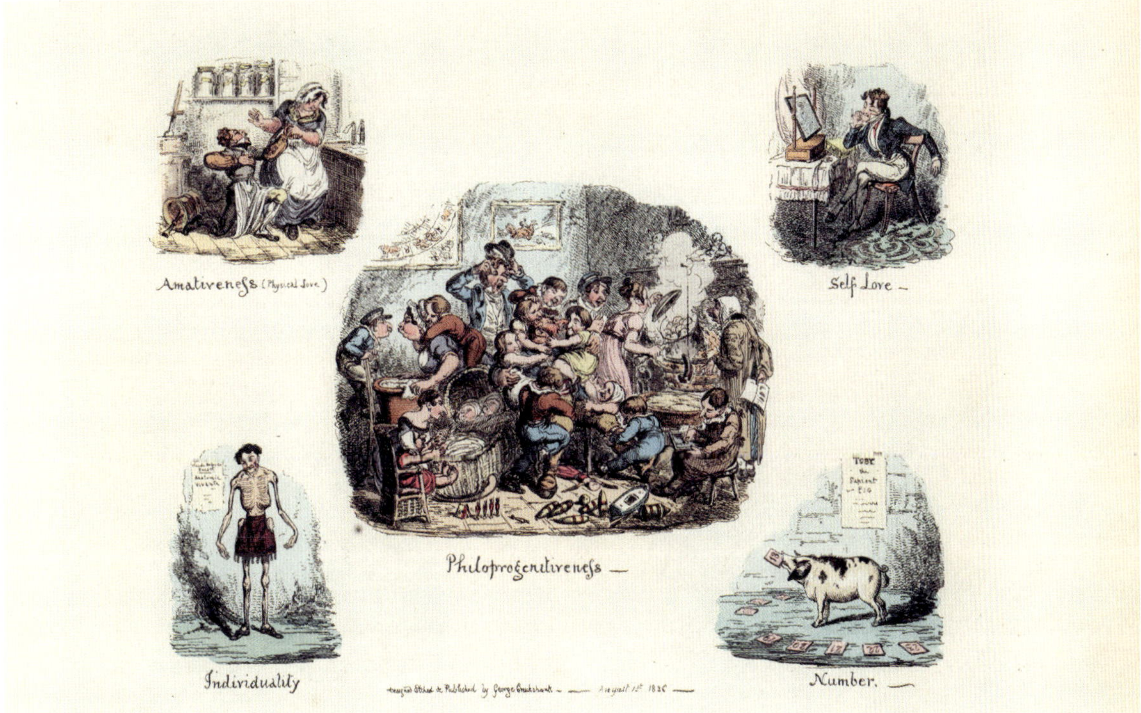

ITEM NO. 43B. Plate 1. "Philoprogenitiveness." This wonderful drawing of a father, mother, and grandmother, with the couple's 16 children, all of whom have a nose inherited from their dad (and their grandma), is a gem.

43B.

Phrenological Illustrations, Or an Artist's View of the Craniological System of Doctors Gall and Spurzheim. By George Cruikshank. London: Published by George Cruikshank, Myddelton Terrace, Pentonville; and Sold by J. Robins and Co., Ivy Lane, Paternoster Row; S. Knights, Sweeting's Alley, Royal Exchange; and G. Humphrey, 24 St. James Street. MDCCCXXVI. Uncolored wrapper; six hand-colored and numbered plates, each with inscription "Designed Etched and Published by George Cruikshank – August 1st 1826."

43C.

Scraps and Sketches. By George Cruikshank. To Be Continued Occasionally. Published by the Author, 22 Myddelton Terrace, Pentonville, and Sold by James Robins & Co., Ivy Lane, Paternoster Row. MDCCCXXVIII. (Uncolored wrapper; six uncolored and unnumbered plates.)

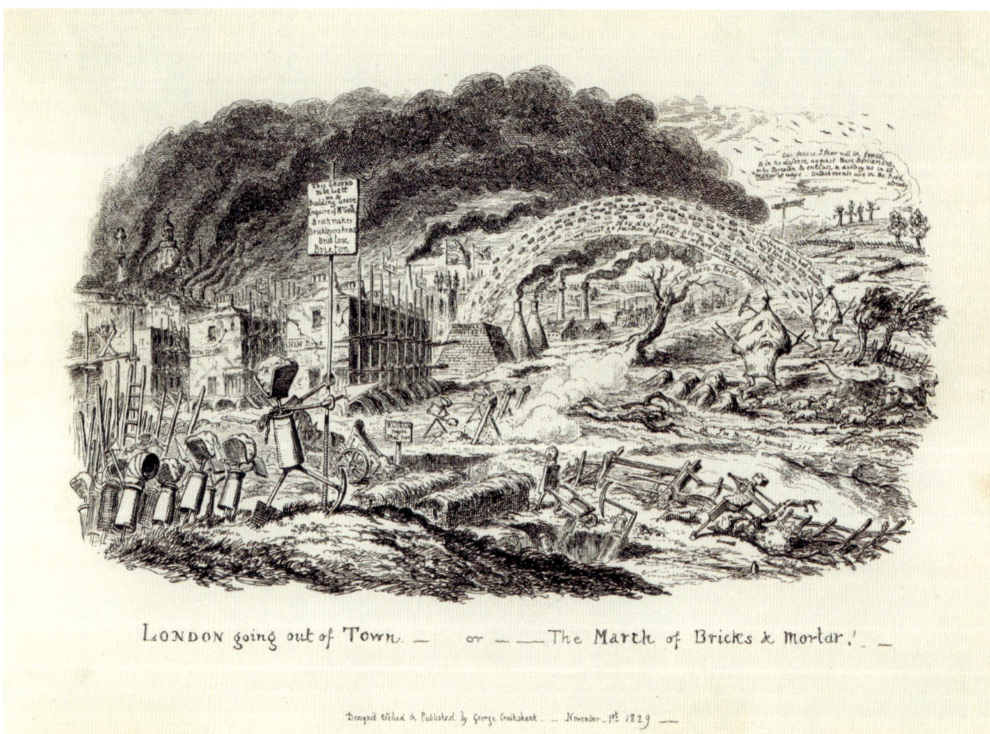

ITEM NO. 43D. Plate 1. "London going out of Town, or the March of Bricks and Mortar."

43D.

Scraps and Sketches. Part the Second. By George Cruikshank. Published by the Author, 22 Myddelton Terrace, Pentonville and Sold by James Robins & Co., Ivy Lane, Paternoster Row. MDCCCXXIX. Uncolored wrapper; six uncolored and unnumbered plates each with inscription "Designed Etched and Published by George Cruikshank – November 1st 1829."

44

Punch and Judy. With Illustrations Designed and Engraved by George Cruikshank. Accompanied by the Dialogue of the Puppet Show, an Account of its Origin, and of Puppet Plays in England. [By John Payne Collier] London: Printed for S. Prowett, 55, Pall Mall. 1828. Twenty-four etched plates including frontispiece, in two states, uncolored and colored on heavy paper indicating that it is from the first issue of the first edition, plus four woodcuts in text plus the title-page vignette. Cohn 150. This best-known puppet play made its first appearance in England in 1662 and had been performed throughout England for many years by "a very old Italian wayfaring puppet-show-man of the name of Piccini." Introduction, p. 74. This book was the play's first publication. The text was recorded by Collier directly from a specially commissioned performance by Piccini, accompanied by Cruikshank, who made his drawings while watching the play.[80]

ITEM NO. 44. Hand-Colored Frontispiece. "Mr. Punch. Etched by George Cruikshank. From the original miniature in the possession of the Publisher. London Pubd by S. Prowett, 55 Pall Mall." See image on page 27.

45

The Life of Napoleon Bonaparte, Late Emperor of the French, King of Italy, Protector of the Confederation of the Rhine, Mediator of the Confederation of Switzerland, &c. &c., his Astonishing Career, etc., with Biographical Memoirs of Contemporary Characters, &c., &c. Edited by W. H. Ireland, Member of the Atheneum of Sciences and Arts at Paris. Embellished with Accurate Views of His Battles, &c. &c. &c., Engraved by G. Cruikshank from the original Designs of Vernet, Denon, &c., executed at Paris by Duplesis Berteaux. Vol. 1. London: Printed and Published by John Fairburn, Broadway, Ludgate Hill. 1823. Four Volumes. Originally published in 64 separate parts, then gathered into four volumes (16 parts per volume). This is the first issue of the first book edition, containing the original 27 plates, 24 of which are hand-colored, all but one of which are foldout.[81]

46

"A Battle of Engravers." Etching signed "George Cruikshank fecit – TW," with engraved title. Tailpiece to "Description of Illustrations," Plate 44, for Thomas Wilson's *A Catalogue Raisonné of the Select Collection of Engravers of an Amateur.* [1828]. Design depicting three pairs of combatants using engraver's tools as weapons. Hogarth attacks Antoine Masson (1636–1700); William Woollett (1735–1785) fights with J. J. Baléchou (1719–1764); behind them Dürer (his monogram on his shield) attacks Marcantonio Raimondi (c. 1480–c. 1530). Among un-

---

80. Ibid., *George Cruikshank's Life,* 1:320.

81. Volumes I–III were published by John Fairburn; Volume IV by John Cumberland. Each volume has an engraved title page, reading: *The Life of Napoleon Bonaparte.* By W. H. Ireland, Esq., Member of the Atheneum of Sciences and Arts at Paris. In Four Volumes – London: Printed for John Cumberland, 19, Ludgate Hill. 1828. I believe this set is a first issue of the first book edition, as it contains the first issue of the printed title page in Volume I, and the engraved title page in each volume gives Cumberland's address as "19 Ludgate Hill," rather than the address Cohn gives for Cumberland's address used on the second issue: "2 Cumberland Terrace, New Town." See Cohn, *George Cruikshank, A Catalogue Raisonné,* 435.

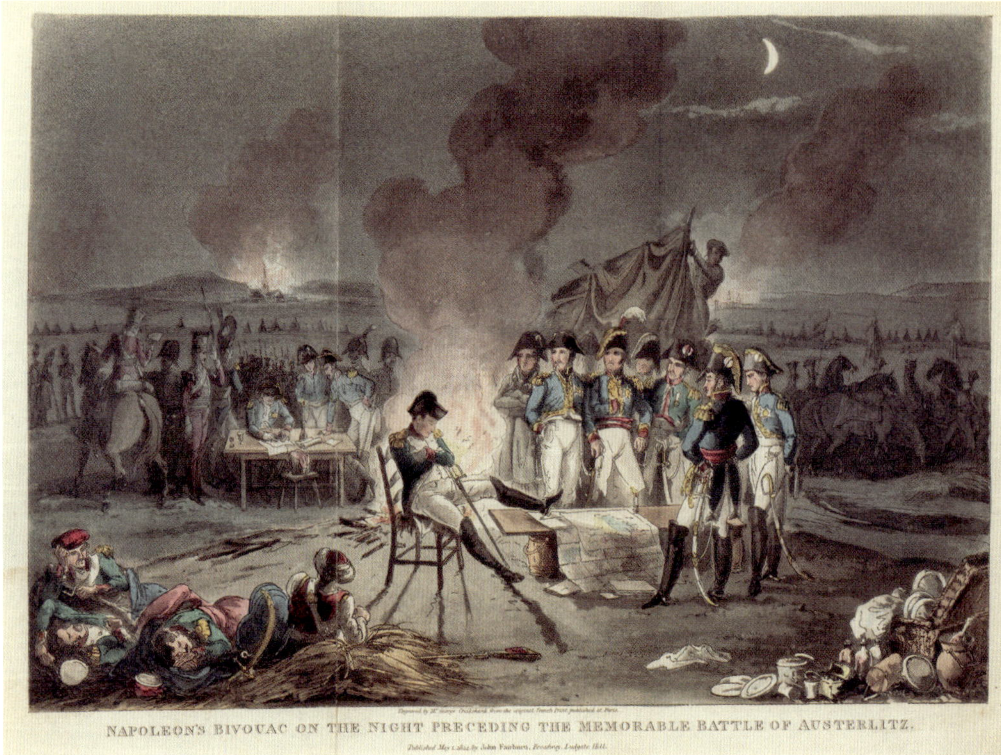

ITEM NO. 45A. Volume II: "Napoleon's Bivouac on the Night Before the Memorable Battle of Austerlitz." Published May 1, 1824, by John Fairburn, Broadway, Ludgate Hill. Engraved by Mr. George Cruikshank from the original French print published at Paris.

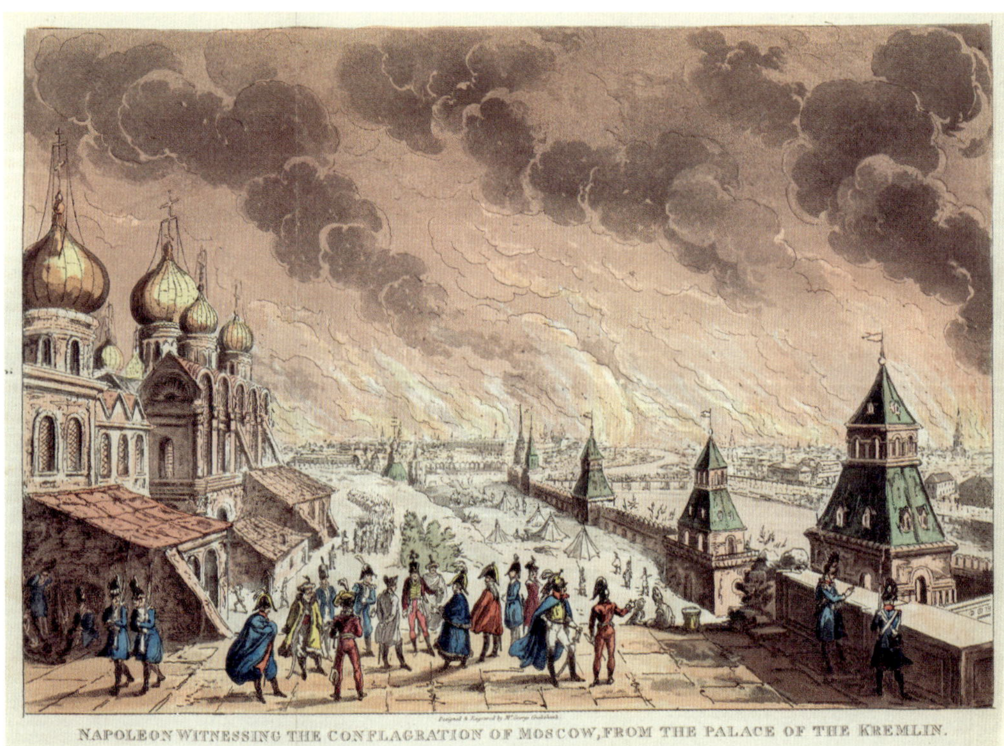

ITEM NO. 45B. Volume III: "Napoleon Witnessing the Conflagration of Moscow, from the Palace of the Kremlin." Published Jan'y 20, 1826, by John Fairburn, Broadway, Ludgate Hill. Designed & Engraved by Mr. George Cruikshank.

identified engravers is a man firing a huge bottle (cannon) of aquafortis supported on a grindstone. Thomas Wilson (1787–1863), a lawyer and print collector, published the catalogue of his collection in 1828, with engravings by Cruikshank, Periam, Hays, Warren, and Howard. He was agent to Lord Portman, and went bankrupt in 1835 largely by investing in one of Portman's unsuccessful ventures. BMS 15616.

47

Three Courses and a Dessert. The Decorations by George Cruikshank. London: Vizetelly, Branston and Co., Fleet Street, 1830. A collection of stories edited by William Clarke. Fifty-five woodcuts designed and cut by Cruikshank, eight of which are full page.

ITEM NO. 47. Vignette of oyster on page 197, tailpiece for "The Native and the Odd Fish." An amusing tale, recounted in West County Irish, of an oyster who describes marvelous doings under the sea to keep a very hungry Mick McGuire from eating him up. Thackeray was enchanted by Cruikshank's numerous woodcuts in this book, saying of the little fellow: "Examine him well; his beard; his pearl, his little round stomach, and his sweet smile. Only oysters know how to smile in this way; cool, gentle, waggish, and yet inexpressibly innocent and winning."[82] See image on page 34.

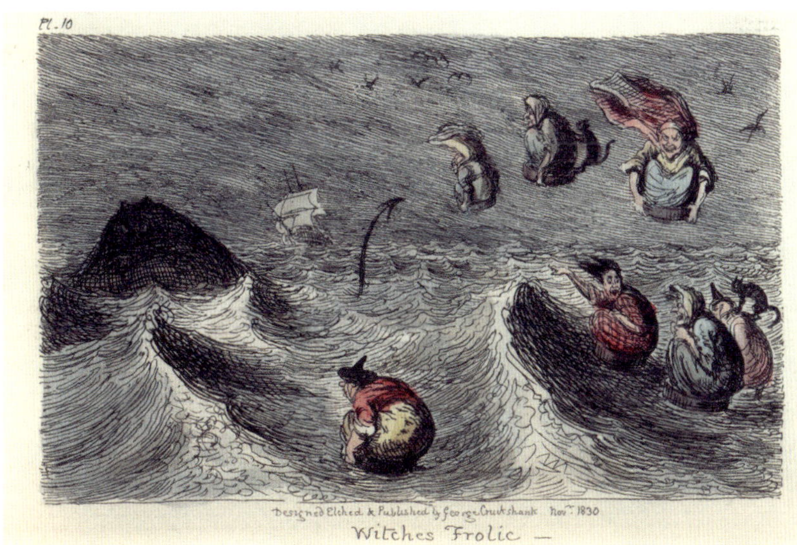

ITEM NO. 48. Plate 10: "Witches Frolic" with hand-coloring.

48

Letters on Demonology and Witchcraft, Addressed to J. G. Lockhart, Esq. By Sir Walter Scott, Bart. London: John Murray, Albemarle Street, MDCCCXXX. Frontispiece by J. Skene, engraved by W. H. Lizars. EXTRA-ILLUSTRATED with 12 engravings in three states (India proof, uncolored, and hand-colored), from the first and second issues of "Twelve Sketches Illustrative of Sir Walter Scott's Demonology and Witchcraft," published for Cruikshank by J. Robins & Co. London. 1830. According to Cohn, the first issue of Cruikshank's plates was only on plain and India paper uncolored; the colored versions here are probably from a reissue of the suite published in 1837 by Charles Tilt. Cohn 188 and 731.

---

82. Patten, *George Cruikshank's Life*, 1:329, 330.

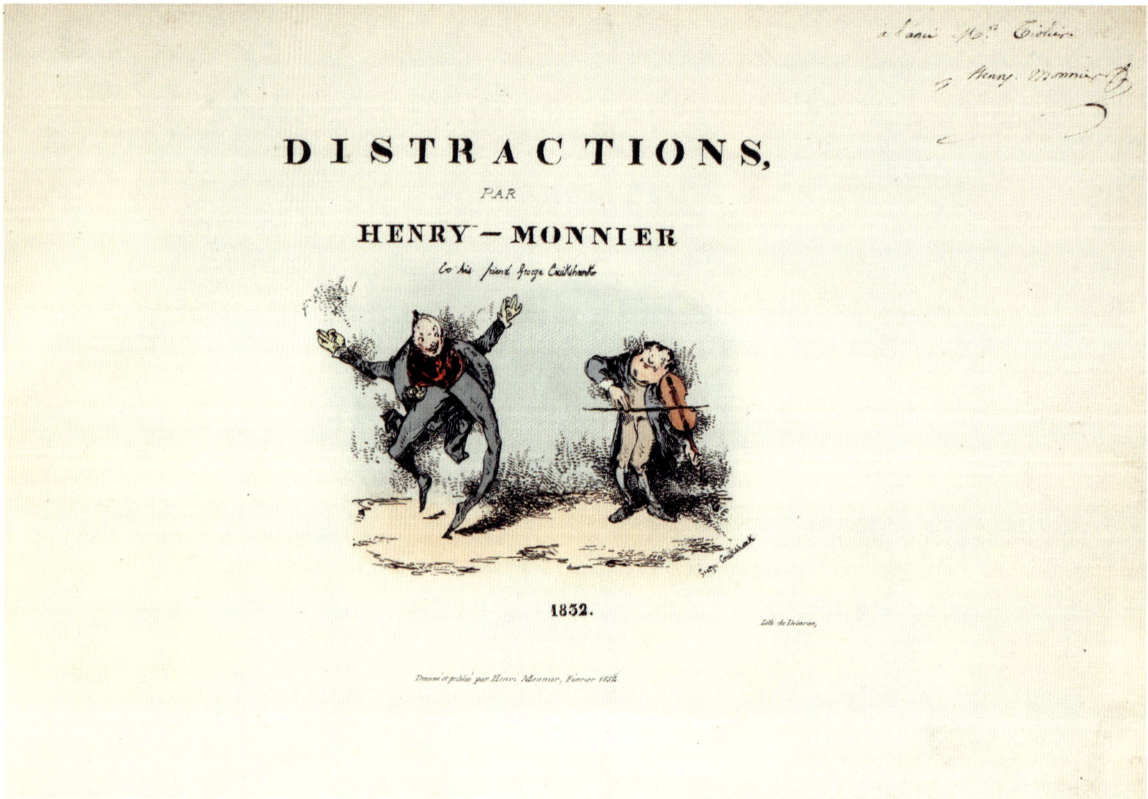

ITEM NO. 49. Title page.

49

Distractions, par Henry Monnier. Paris. Paulin, Libraire-Editeur. Place de la Bourse. Delarue, Imprimeur Lithographe, 16, Rue Norte Dames des Victoires. London. Colnaghi, Son and Co. Pall-Mall East. 1832. Title page: "To his friend George Cruikshank." [With a rather crude color lithograph of a Cruikshank-like design of two elves with what looks like a copy of George Cruikshank's signature]. Lith: de Delarue, Dessiné et Publié par Henry Monnier, Février 1832. Autograph dedication: "À l'ami M. Tiolien. Henry Monnier." Album. Six leaves with four sketches of amusing hand-colored lithographs on each. I find no counterpart in any of Cruikshank's works for the image on Monnier's title page. Monnier (1799–1877) visited Cruikshank twice in London during the 1820s. (Title page not in Cohn.)

50

"A Fable for Ministers, The Grey, Its Rider – & The Wild Fire." Published by Thos. McLean, 26, Haymarket, May 12, 1832. A. Ducote's Lithogy, St Marks Lane. Hand-colored lithograph with lithographed signature "HB" [John Doyle] in picture, and embossed seal on white paper below the print.

51

Figaro in London, Vols. I, II, III, and IV. For the Years 1832–1835. London: Printed by W. Molineux, Rolls Buildings, Fetter Lane. Published by William Strange, 21, Paternoster Row. Two Volumes (Volumes I and II bound together, III and IV bound together). Weekly satirical newspaper consisting of four pages (two leaves) each, launched in December 1831, running through December 1838. The paper's original editor was Gilbert Abbott à Beckett (1811–1856); Henry Mayhew became editor between 1835 and 1836, after which à Beckett took over again.[83] Robert Seymour became *Figaro*'s primary artist. He designed the logo and 300 humorous drawings and political caricatures, all wood engravings, to accompany the rather mundane, political topics written by à Beckett. In 1834, the editor suffered heavy financial losses, refused to pay Robert Seymour, and launched a public campaign libeling him. Seymour resigned, returning to the periodical only when Mayhew became editor shortly before the artist's death in 1836.

52

The School Master Abroad. By One of the Old School. With illustrations by R. Seymour. Published by Thos. McLean, 26, Haymarket, Sepr. 22, 1834; Ducote & Stevens, Lithographers, 70, St. Martins Lane, London. Nine numbered and hand-colored lithographs intended as a mild satire on Lord Brougham and his educational schemes. (Surely also intended to mimic the straight-laced Dr. Syntax.) The letterpress is Seymour's as well as the drawings. J.C. Hotten [1867], p. 6. This gorgeous album of lithographs was preceded by *The Schoolmaster at Home*, published by Benjamin Steill in June 1832, also a satire on Brougham's views on education.

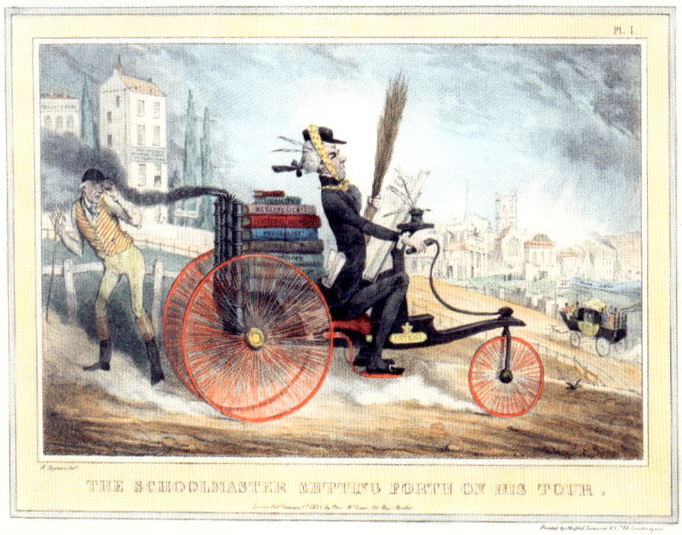

ITEM NO. 52. Plate I: "The School Master Setting Forth on His Tour," R. Seymour del. London: Pubd. January 1st, 1832, by Thos McLean, 26 Hay-Market. Printed by Meifred Lemercier & Co., 24 Leicester Square.

---

83. As proclaimed in the opening editorial, the title was adopted in order to build on the success of the French satirical daily *Le Figaro,* founded five years before. Figaro was the hero of Pierre-Augustin Caron de Beaumarchais's play *Le Mariage de Figaro*, which poked fun at privilege. Seymour's logo represents a barber (Figaro's profession) attacking one of several effigy heads (block heads) mounted on stands. At its peak, the circulation of *Figaro in London* ran to 70,000 copies.

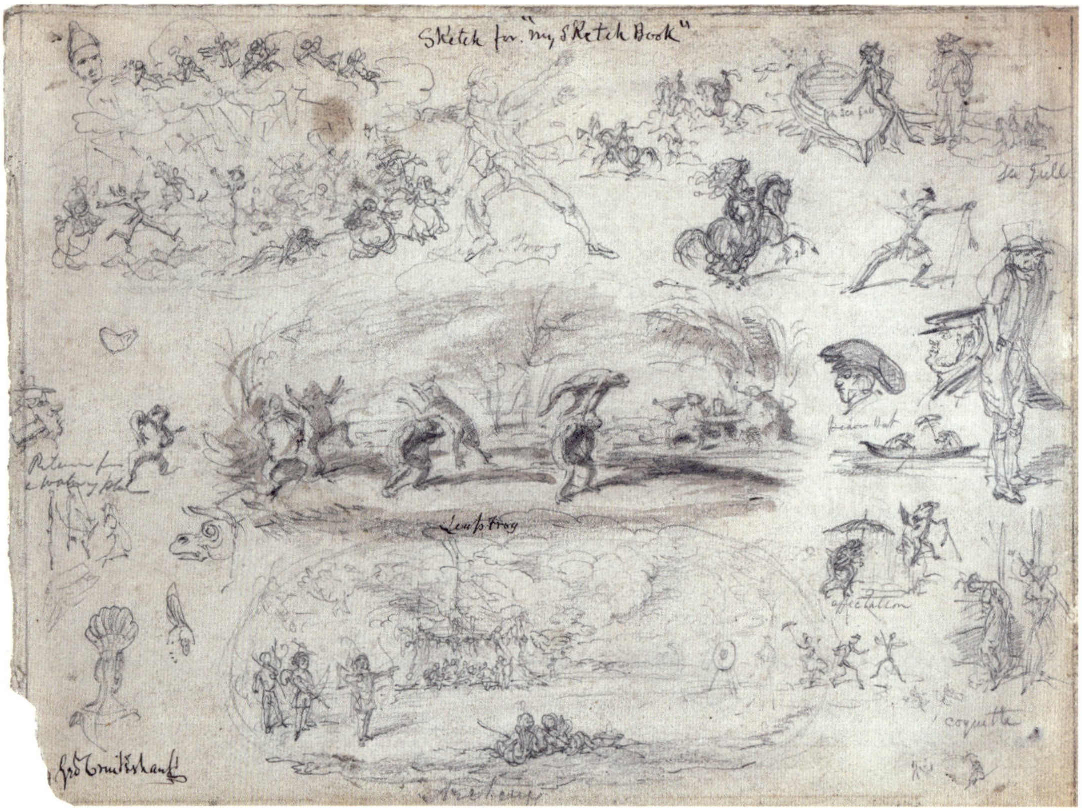

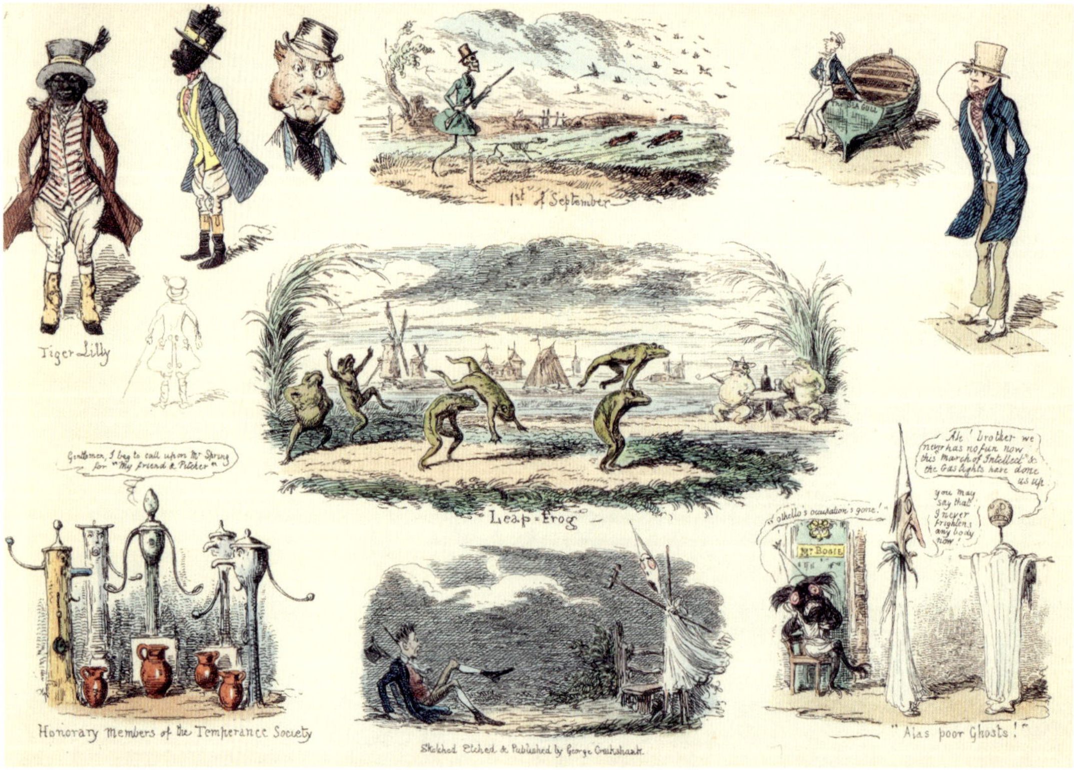

ITEM NOS. 53A & 53B. Plate of hand-colored vignettes with the middle one entitled "Leap Frog," with a sheet of original penciled sketches from the Zukor Album, including the one for the "Leap Frog" plate.

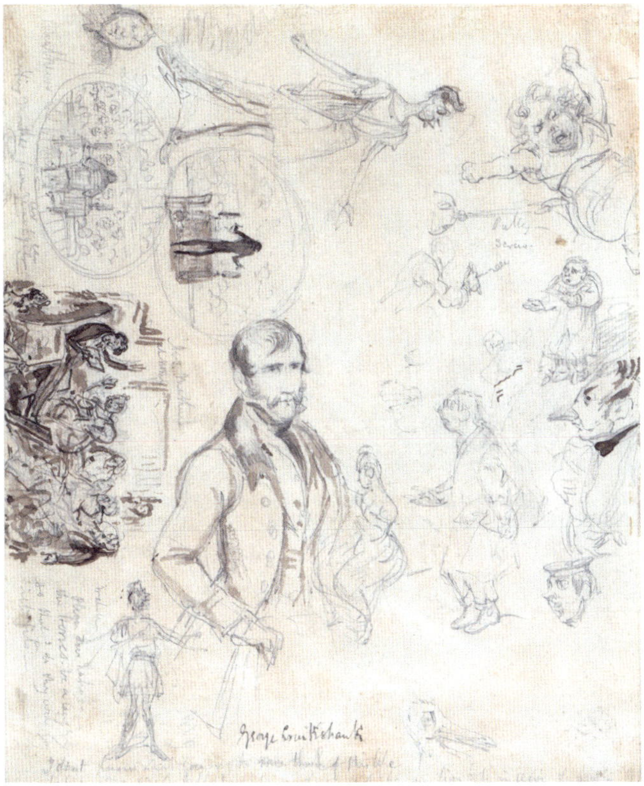

ITEM NO. 53C. A sheet from the Zukor Album with penciled self-portrait by Cruikshank, surrounded with pencil, pen & ink, and wash sketches, with handwritten notes.

53

Volume 1 of My Sketch Book, Designed, Etched & Published by George Cruikshank. 23 Myddleton Terrace, Pentonville & Sold by Charles Tilt, 86 Fleet Street. Dec. 1st, 1834. Album containing engraved title page and 36 etched plates with many hand-colored caricature sketches on each, making puns and fun of everyday life, issued in nine publications, four plates each, in tan wrappers, all of which, front and back, are bound in after the plates. Binding by Rivière and Son.

54

A Comic Alphabet, Designed Etched & Published by George Cruikshank. No. 23 Myddleton Terrace, Pentonville. 1837. Second edition, with 24 hand-colored etchings, each separated by a leaf, and yellow wrappers designed by Cruikshank, the rear with a portrait of Charles Tilt (in his bookshop surrounded by Cruikshank's illustrated books), with a T at the top of the page, bound in front and rear. The coloring is superb. First issued in 1836 as 24 uncolored etchings on a single sheet folded into the yellow wrappers. Cohn 189.

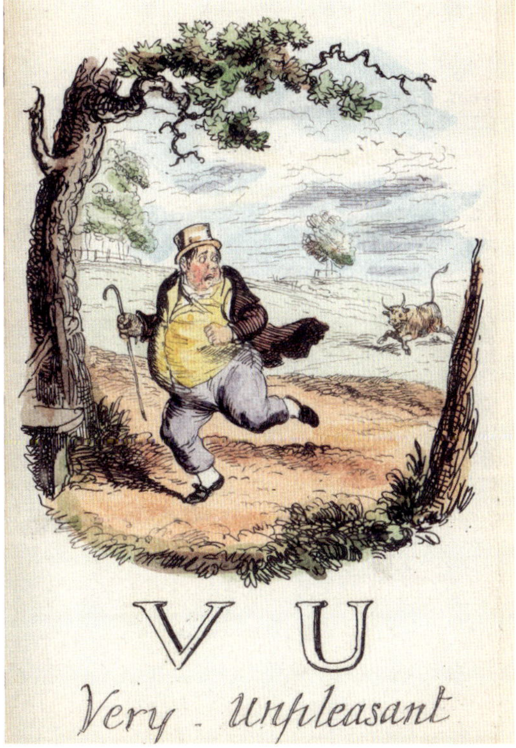

ITEM NO. 54. "V U – Very Unpleasant."

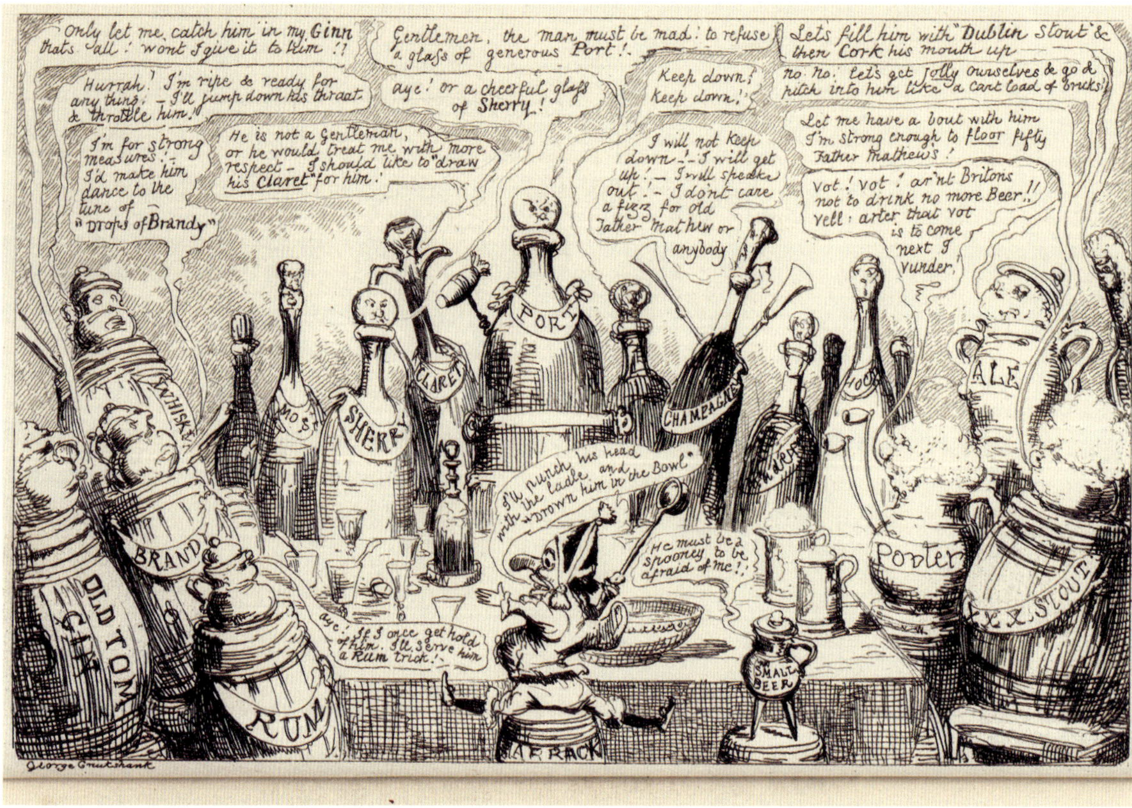

ITEM NO. 55B. 1844: "January: Wine in a Ferment, and Spirits in Hot Water," illustrating "The Great Anti-Temperance Meeting" article.

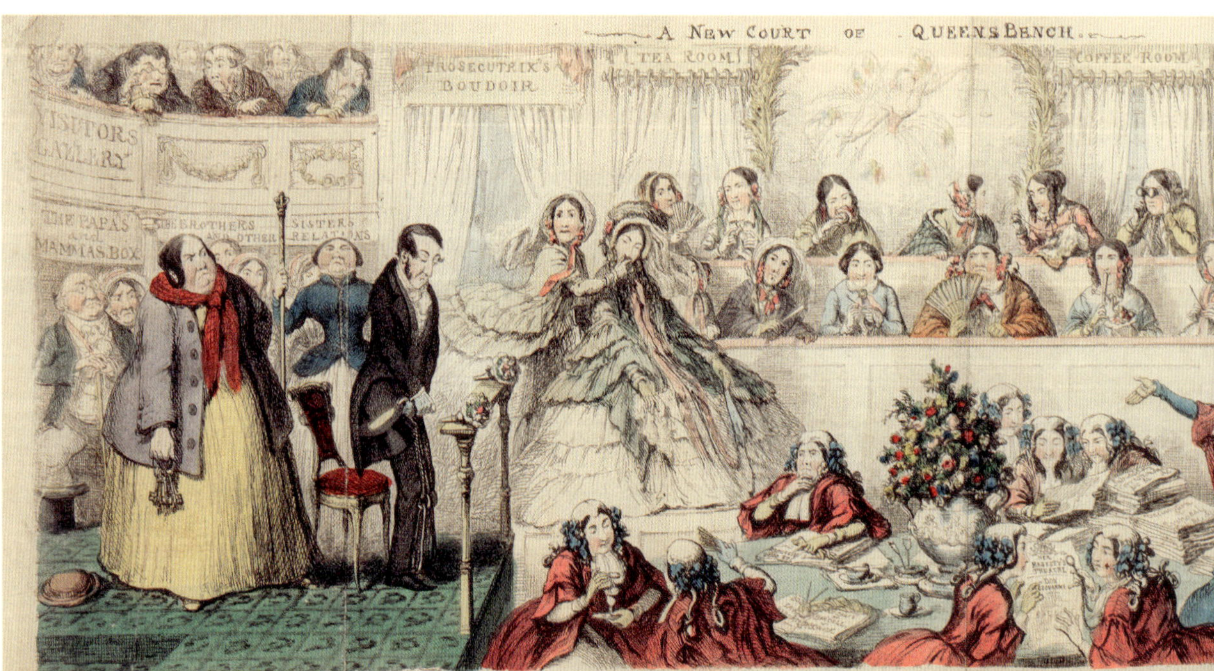

ITEM NO. 55C. 1850: Colored folding frontispiece: "A New Court of Queen's Bench. As It Ought to Be – Or – The Ladies Trying a Contemptible Scoundrel for a 'Breach of Promise.'"

55

The Comic Almanack, For 1835: An Ephemeris in Jest and Earnest, containing "All Things Fitting for such a Work." By Rigdum Funnidos, Gent. [Thackeray, Albert Smith, Gilbert à Beckett, the Brothers Mayhew.] Adorned with a Dozen of "Righte Merrie" Cuts, Pertaining to the Months, Sketched and Etched By George Cruikshank. London, Printed for Charles Tilt, Bibliopolist, in Fleet Street. Vizetelly, Brandston and Co., Printers, Fleet Street. Complete set of 19 almanacs in original wrappers published 1835–1853 in nine volumes. All volumes bound by Zaehnsdorf; first volume has book plate of Donald S. Tuttle. The 1835–1847 Almanacks each had 12 plates: 1848 (6); 1849 (5); and 1850–1853 (7).

By 1842, Charles Tilt had taken on his young employee, David Bogue, as partner. Thus, the Almanacks for 1842 and 1843 were published by "Tilt and Bogue, Bibliopolists in Fleet Street," and after 1844, when Tilt had retired, the publisher became "David Bogue, Bibliopolist in Fleet Street," for the remaining editions. The original printer was Vizetelly, Branston and Co. James Henry Vizetelly wrote most of the Almanack's letterpress and collaborated with Cruikshank on the ideas for the plates until his death in 1838. Thackeray was then brought in to write several pieces for the 1839 and 1840 editions. Cruikshank had difficulty thereafter finding writers to provide the wit. James Henry Vizetelly's son, Henry Vizetelly, became the Almanack's printer with his brother James in 1848; in 1850, this changed to "Henry Vizetelly, Printer and Engraver, Gough Square, Fleet Street, London," who remained the printer for the last four Almanacks.

ITEM NO. 55A. 1835: "March," picturing Charles Tilt's print shop on Fleet Street with the proprietor in the doorway. See image on page 18.

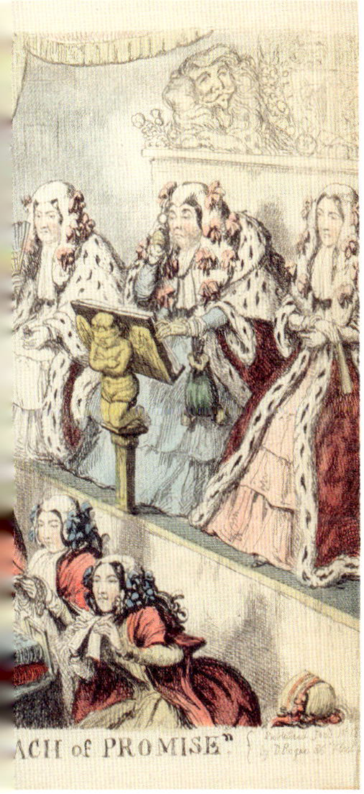

56

The Comic Almanack. No title page, n.d. Small contemporary album with 36 plates by George Cruikshank, published one per month for the years 1836–1838.

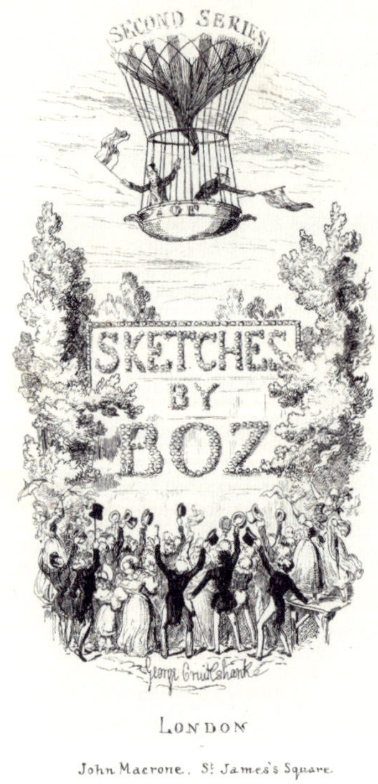

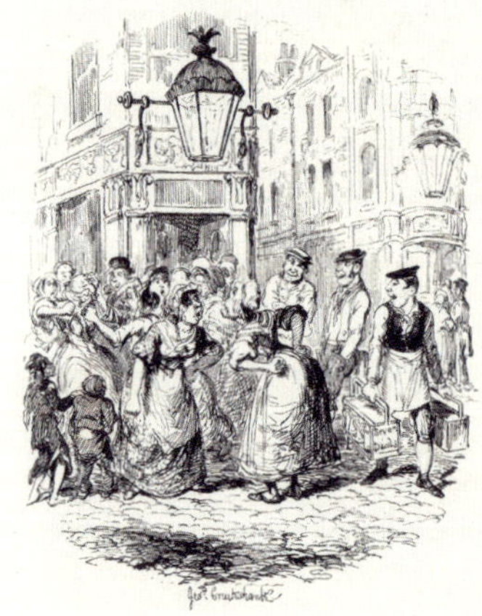

First proof
Geo Cruikshank

ITEM NO. 58B. First Proof – Second Series: Title page with facing etching.

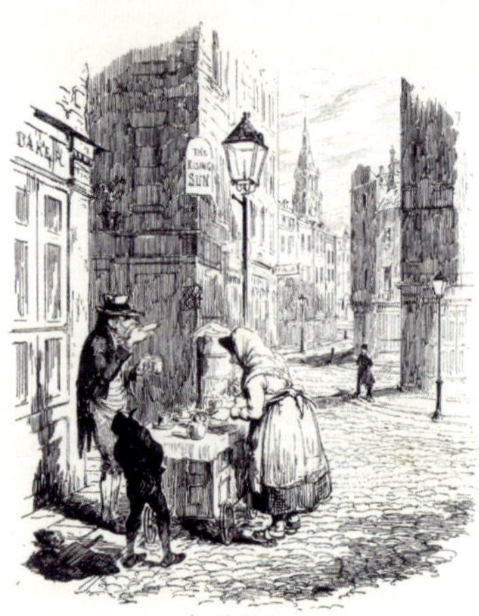

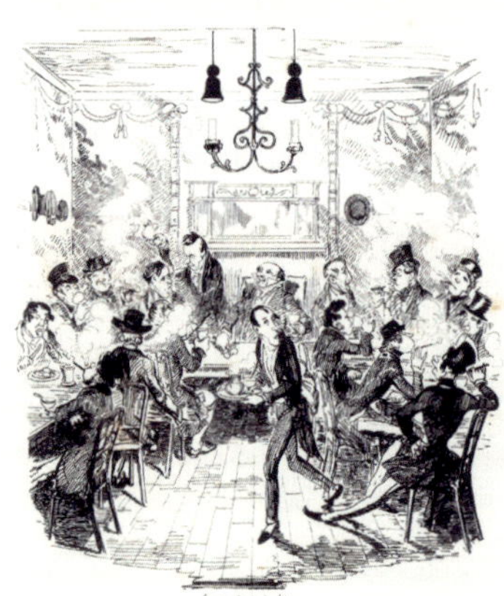

First proof Geo Cruikshank

ITEM NO. 58C. First Proof – Second Series: "The Streets, Morning" and "Free and Easy," the one plate omitted from the 1839 volume of both series.

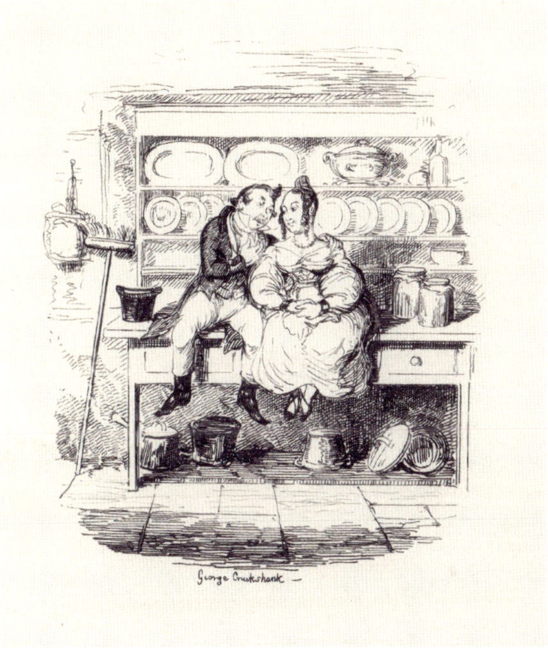

ITEM NO. 57.
Volume II:
Frontispiece: "Mr.
Gabriel Parsons'
Courtship."

1835–1840: THE ARRIVAL OF MR. DICKENS

57

Sketches by "Boz" Illustrative of Every-Day Life, and Every-Day People. In Two Volumes. Illustrations by George Cruikshank. London: John Macrone, St. James Square. MDCCCXXXVI. First edition, first issue in original green cloth bindings.

58

Sketches by Boz. Both Series. Proofs of the Etchings by George Cruikshank. 1836. Album assembled by Henry Bruton (1843–1920), a successful Gloucester auctioneer and preeminent collector of Dickens and Cruikshank. The Album includes the original pencil drawing for the frontispiece of *Sketches by Boz, Second Series*, printed title page, and 28 etched proof plates before letters on India paper (two images per sheet as printed), mounted on 14 leaves and matted. Each of the 12 proof images for the *Second Series* is labeled in pencil "First Proof" with Cruikshank's signature. Also included is a proof for the frontispiece for the 1852 edition of *Sketches by Boz*, and two states of the wrapper designed by Cruikshank and cut on wood by Jackson for *Sketches*, both *Series*, sold in parts by Chapman and Hall from November 1937 through June 1839. Bruton's ink signature is on the first blank page of the Album.

The Album is accompanied by an autograph letter from Bruton to B. B. McGeorge, Esq., dated June 10, 1906, thanking the latter for sending him a copy of the catalogue of McGeorge's collection. It gives fascinating evidence of both men's collecting habits and the provenance of the contents of the Album, saying in part:

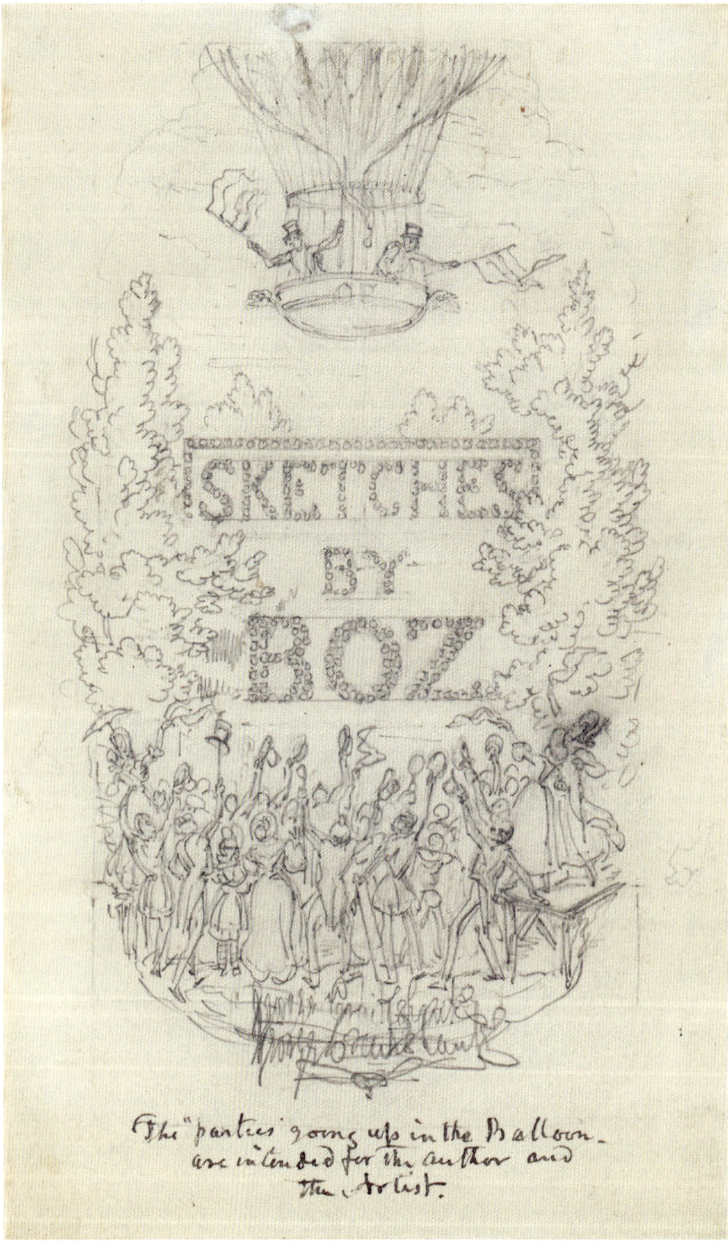

ITEM NO. 58A. Original pencil drawing for the title page of *Sketches by Boz, Second Series,* published by John Macrone in December 1836, signed at the bottom twice in pencil "George Cruikshank," with a note below in pen in Cruikshank's hand: "The parties going up in the balloon are intended for the author and the artist."

What a glorious collection & how marvellously [*sic*] rich in part books! I am very glad to know on whose shelves some of my choicest GCk's repose. Forgive my being critical – but why have you omitted any reference to the proof of the wrapper of the parts which I inserted in the vol of proofs to *Sketches by Boz*? I looked upon this wrapper as a most interesting item – it was the only one known to me. It formed part of a collection of woodcuts cut by Jackson[84] & was brought to Robson by a member of his family. I called at the shop shortly after the collection had been purchased & was delighted to get it of Robson for £2.20.

84. John Jackson (1801–1848) was a British wood engraver, apprenticed to Thomas Bewick. After a quarrel with his master, Jackson went to London and worked for the wood engraver William Harvey. Wikipedia, s.v. "John Jackson (engraver)," accessed June 9, 2020, https://en.wikipedia.org/wiki/John_Jackson_(engraver).

59

Sketches by Boz Illustrative of Every-Day Life and Every-Day People. With Forty Illustrations by George Cruikshank. New Edition, Complete. London: Chapman and Hall, 186, Strand, 1839. First edition, first issue of the first and second series complete in one volume in original blind-stamped brown cloth binding. After obtaining the copyright for both *Serie*s of *Sketches* from John Macrone in 1837, Chapman and Hall published both in 20 monthly parts from November 1837 through June 1839. Cruikshank designed the pink paper wrapper for each part, enlarged the plates (except for "The Free and Easy," which was discarded), and created 13 new illustrations. In May 1839, Chapman and Hall published the parts complete in one volume (present here) with all 40 of Cruikshank's etchings. For some of the first issue of the new volume, they used unsold copies of the parts, which can be identified by stab holes used to sew the parts.[85] This copy has the stab holes visible in a number of places.

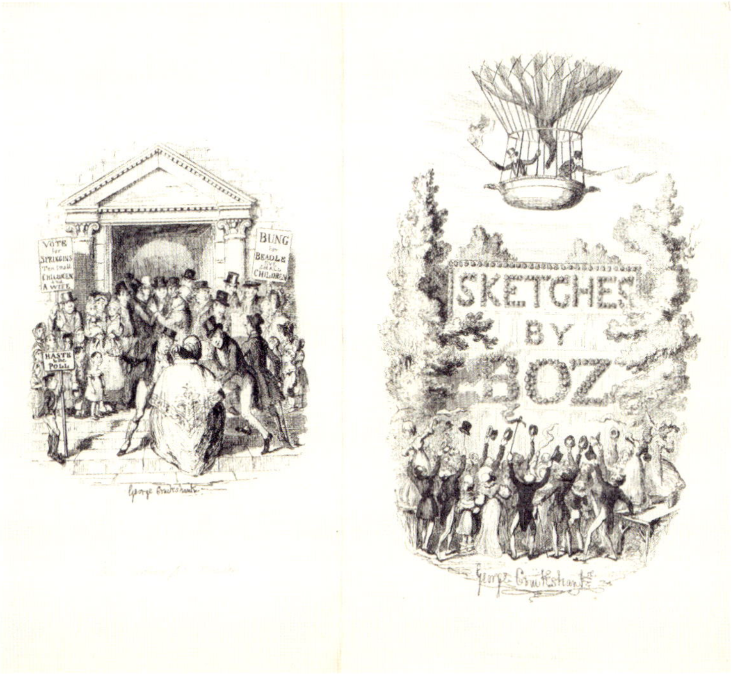

ITEM NO. 59A. Title page with balloon and "The Election of Beadle" as frontispiece. The title page was created by Cruikshank for *Sketches by Boz, Second Series,* published in December 1836; "The Election of Beadle" was the frontispiece to *Sketches by Boz,* First Series, published in February 1836.

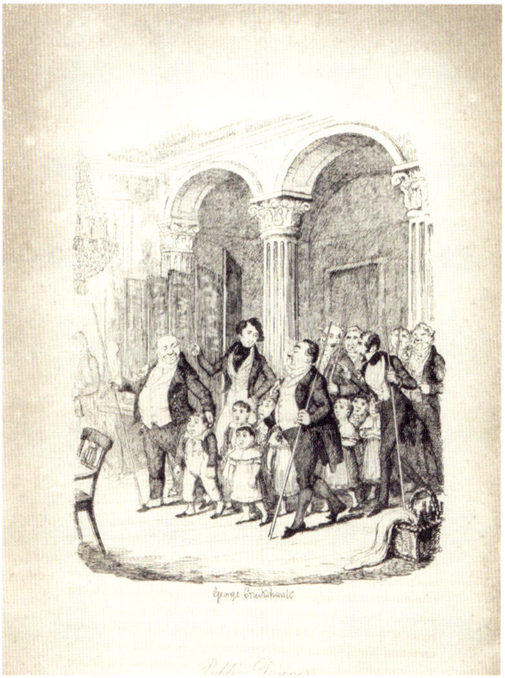

ITEM NO. 59B. Public Dinners, p. 175. Attending a charitable dinner is far more amusing than having to sit through a company or political dinner, according to the text. Here we see Dickens and Cruikshank attending a charitable dinner to support "Indigent Orphans' Friends' Benevolent Institution in the company of Messrs. Chapman and Hall.*
(Note the stab holes in left-hand margin.)

---

85. John C. Eckel, *The First Editions of the Writings of Charles Dickens and Their Values, A Bibliography* (London: Chapman & Hall, Ltd., 1913), 19.

* Ibid., 18.

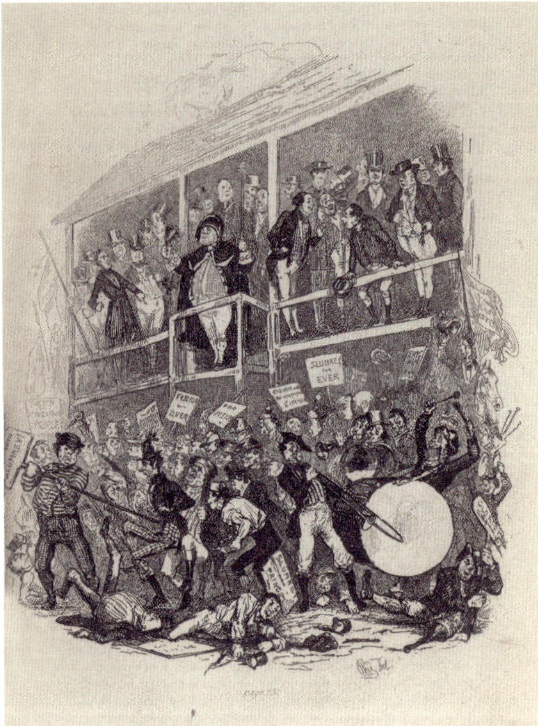

ITEM NO. 60. "The Election" by Phiz, p. 132.

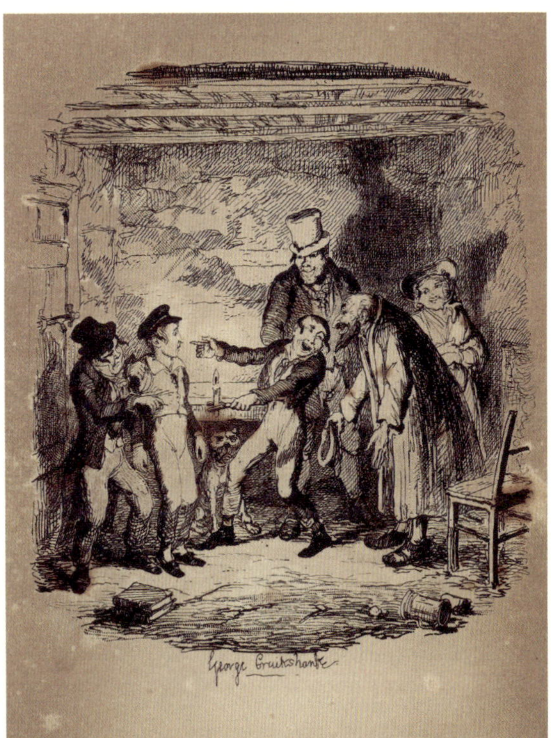

ITEM NO. 62A. Volume I: Frontispiece: "Oliver's reception by Fagin and the boys."

60

The Posthumous Papers of the Pickwick Club, by Charles Dickens. With forty-three illustrations by R. Seymour and Hablot Browne. London: Chapman and Hall, 186, Strand. MDCCCXXXVII. First book edition. EXTRA-ILLUSTRATED. Includes engraved title page signed "Phiz fecit" and dated 1836; two plates by Robert William Buss (a wood engraver, not an etcher) (one in facsimile); an extra suite of plates by Thomas Onwyhn (1814–1886); and two states of many of Phiz's etchings. First published in parts from March 1836–November 1837.

61

Sketches by Seymour. Vol. I–Vol. V. Published by G.S. Tregear, 96 Cheapside, London. Bound in one volume. 1834–1836. Thirty-six lithographs on tinted paper in each volume for a total of 185 plates. In 1834, as he was just gaining recognition as a fine comic artist, Seymour launched a series of humorous lithographs depicting expeditions of overequipped and undertrained Cockneys attempting to acquire the sporting acumen of the upper classes. Presumably, these deft and amusing satires lay the groundwork for Seymour's proposal for the *Pickwick* book, which he took to Chapman and Hall in late 1835 (see discussion on p. 21).

62

Oliver Twist or, the Parish Boy's Progress. By "Boz." In Three Volumes. London: Richard Bentley, New Burlington Street. 1838. First issue of the first edition, without the list of illustrations, having "Boz" on the title page in all three volumes and the "Fireside" plate at the end of Vol. III. Eckel 52–54. In original boards. First issued in monthly installments in *Bentley's Miscellany* from February 1837 through April 1839.

ITEM NO. 62B. Volume III: "Fagin in the Condemned Cell," p. 297. See image on page 22.

63

Two issues of *Bentley's Miscellany*. Edited by Boz. Illustrated by George Cruikshank. No. XXIII. November 1, 1838 and No. XXIV. December 1, 1838. New York. Jemima M. Lewer, Broadway, Corner of Pine Street. First American Edition. In original wrappers. Each issue contains two chapters of *Oliver Twist* (Book the Third – Chapter the Fifth and Sixth in Vol. XXIII; Book the Third – Chapter the Seventh and Eighth in Vol. XXIV). Each chapter has one Cruikshank etching.

64

Cruikshank's Water Colours, with Introduction by Joseph Grego, published by A. & C. Black. London. MCMIII, containing three suites of the original watercolor drawings for the illustrations for *Oliver Twist, The Miser's Daughter,* and *The History of the Irish Rebellion.* The set of 13 plates for *Oliver Twist* was redrawn and recolored by Cruikshank in 1866 as a commission for his friend, F. W. Cozens.

65

Memoirs of Joseph Grimaldi, Edited by "Boz." With Illustrations by George Cruikshank. In Two Volumes. London: Richard Bentley, New Burlington Street. 1838. First edition, first issue. Twelve etchings by Cruikshank, 28 pages of adverts and a 7-page essay by Bentley entitled "The Standard Novels" in the rear of Vol. II. TOGETHER WITH AUTOGRAPH LETTER FROM GRIMALDI to Cruikshank: "I have for the present changed my mind relative to having my portrait painted. When (?) I again alter my opinion will let you know. Yours ? J. Grimaldi. 33 Southhampton St. Pentonville." Penciled notation below: [Grimaldi] "died 31 May, 1837." Joseph Grimaldi (1778–1837) was an English actor and comedian, so well known on the London comic stage that the role of Clown became known as "Joey," and both the nickname and Grimaldi's whiteface makeup became the hallmark of the classic clown.[86] After his death, Richard Bentley bought the rights to his memoirs, asking Dickens to edit them and Cruikshank to illustrate. The book was produced during the period of intense disputes between Dickens and Bentley. Dickens later said that he agreed to edit *Grimaldi* "chiefly to please Cruikshank," who had known and admired the comic artist.[87]

66

The Loving Ballard of Lord Bateman, Illustrated by George Cruikshank. London: Charles Tilt, Fleet Street, and Mustapha Syriad, Constantinople. MDCCCXXXIX. Eleven woodcuts by Cruikshank. Text of the *Ballard* is on single leaves opposite each of the cuts; there are nine pages of Notes at the end and six pages of adverts for Tilt's publications. Original green cloth over

86. Wikipedia, s.v. "Joseph Grimaldi," accessed June 10, 2020, https://en.wikipedia.org/wiki/Joseph_Grimaldi.
87. Patten, *George Cruikshank's Life,* 2:59, 68.

board wrapper in a black morocco box by Zaehnsdorf. Cruikshank was famous for singing the *Ballard* (about a dandy lord's romantic adventure in Turkey recited by a cockney dustman) at many an evening with friends, particularly when the claret flowed plentifully. In 1839, he decided to write it up and illustrate it for publication. By that time, Cruikshank's party performance had become so beloved that Dickens took to performing it as well; and chance would have it that, just at this time, Thackeray, inspired by Dickens's rendition, also undertook to illustrate it for publication. When he discovered that Cruikshank was planning to publish his own rendition, he withdrew from the fray; Dickens joined the fun, and it was published by Cruikshank's publisher, Charles Tilt, with Cruikshank's woodcuts, Thackeray's text, and Dickens's Preface and notes.[88]

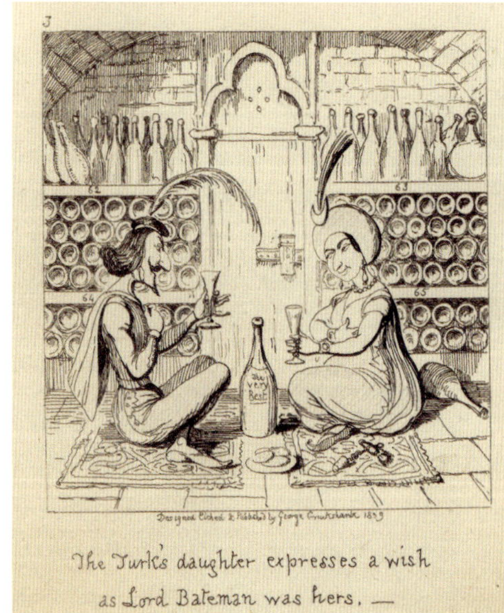

ITEM NO. 66. Plate 3: "The Turk's daughter expresses a wish as Lord Bateman was hers–" Designed Etched & Published by George Cruikshank 1839.

67

Bentley's Miscellany. Ingoldsby Legends: By Thomas Ingoldsby [Richard Harris Barham]. Illustrated by George Cruikshank and John Leech. 1837–1845. This volume contains each of the 41 *Legends* as first printed in *Bentley's Miscellany* from 1837 through 1845 (Volumes I–XVIII), illustrated sporadically with 12 etchings: eight by Cruikshank, three by Leech, and one by Robert Buss. There is a title page with the above description of this odd volume; an "Ingoldsby Legends – Contents" page listing the titles of each of the *Legends*, the illustrations, and their artists in this volume; and a Table of Contents for Volume IX to help explain the presentation of the book. It also includes (i) two original wrappers of the *Miscellany* from this period, both designed by Cruikshank: No. III, March 1, 1837 (when edited by Dickens) and No. LVI, August 2, 1841 (when edited by Ainsworth); (ii) a three-page article entitled "The Rev. Richard Harris Barham. Author of the 'Ingoldsby Legends,' " with etched portrait of Barham from a drawing by Richard Lane, from Volume XVIII of the *Miscellany;* (iii) an elaborate etching designed by Cruikshank for the frontispiece of the 1870 edition of the *Legends*; and finally (iv) 39 pages of advertisements for Richard Bentley's publications, dating mostly from 1841.[89] Binding by Tout. The author, Richard Barham (1788–1845), was a cleric in the Church of England and a much honored friend of both Bentley and Cruikshank. The *Legends* were enormously popular, went through many editions, and were illustrated by many artists.

---

88. Ibid., 2:104, 105.

89. Based on the volume's title page, the etching for the 1870 edition, and the 39 pages of adverts at the end, it appears that this compilation was prepared by Bentley himself a year before he died in 1871. Cohn does not refer to this compilation (which may be unique) or to the serialization of the *Legends* in the *Miscellany.* He records its first publication as entitled *The Ingoldsby Legends, or Mirth and Marvels*, published by Bentley as the *First Series* in 1840, *Second Series*, in 1842, and *Third Series* in 1847. Cohn, *George Cruikshank, A Catalogue Raisonné,* 50. The description of the 1864 edition is at Cohn 51; the 1870 edition is at Cohn 52.

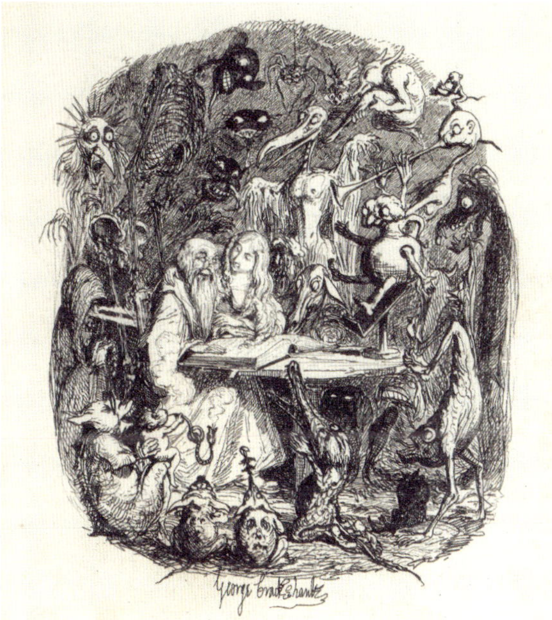

ITEM NO. 67A. Plate at page 100: "Saint Anthony." Signed George Cruikshank. London: Richard Bentley, Jany 1, 1838. [Etching on copper.]

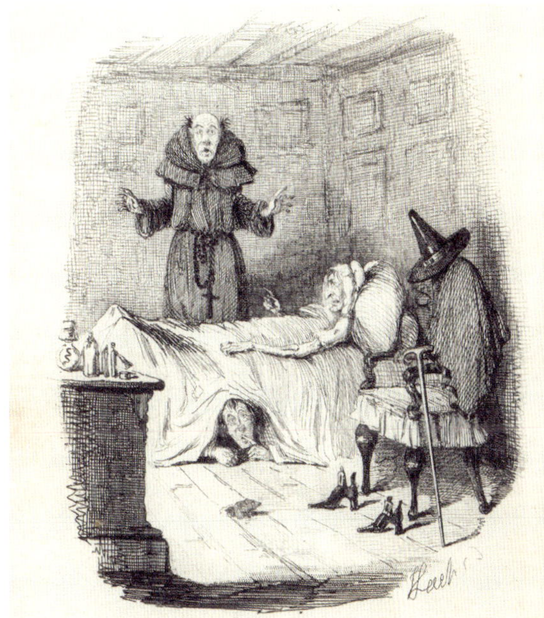

ITEM NO. 67B. Plate at page 86: "The Confession." Signed J. Leech. London: Richard Bentley, 1841. [Etching on copper.]

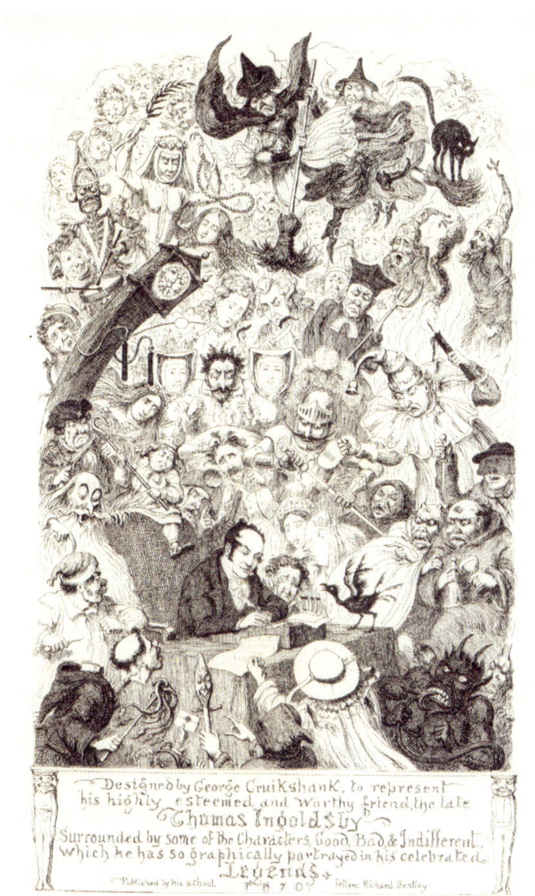

ITEM NO. 67C. Frontispiece designed by George Cruikshank for the 1870 edition "to represent his highly esteemed and Worthy friend, the late Thomas Ingoldsby – Surrounded by some of the Characters, Good, Bad & Indifferent, which he so graphically portrayed in his celebrated Legends. Published by his school fellow, Richard Bentley. 1870." Cruikshank designed this frontispiece for Bentley a year before the publisher died, as a peace offering for their disputes dating back to 1839–1843.*

* Ibid., 52; Patten, *George Cruikshank's Life,* 2:422–424.

68

The Ingoldsby Legends, or Mirth and Marvels, By Thomas Ingoldsby, Esq. With Sixty Illustrations by George Cruikshank [24], John Leech [6] and John Tenniel [30]. London, Richard Bentley, Publisher in Ordinary to Her Majesty. 1864. Binding by Bayntun.

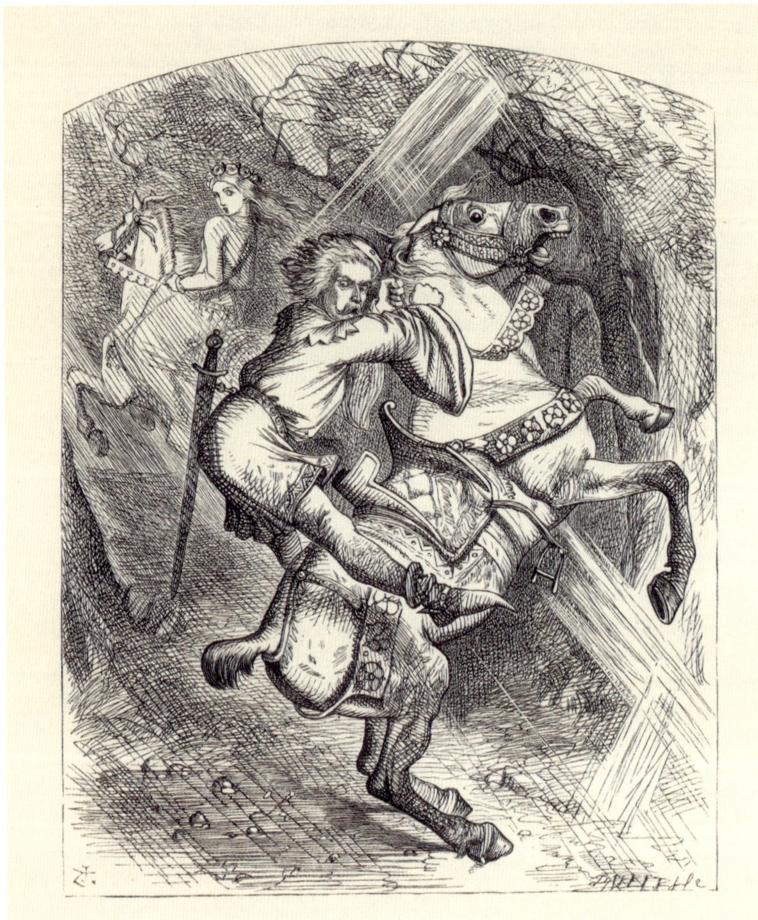

ITEM NO. 68. Tenniel's illustration for "The Blasphemer's Warning," p. 159. [Etching on steel.] Note how Tenniel represents a whole new generation of illustrators: less caricature, more realism.

69

An Essay on the Genius of George Cruikshank. By W. M. Thackeray, Illustrated. [1840]. A reprint of the 60-page article published in *The Westminster Review,* Volume XXXIV, Number 1, 1840, written by Thackeray. Printed by W & C Yates. EXTRA-ILLUSTRATED with 45 of Cruikshank's etchings dating between 1811 and 1840. Many are dated in pencil below the image. Portrait of GCk on title page by F. W. Pailthorpe, the same artist who etched Cruikshank's self-portrait bound in to my edition of *Life in London.* See Item No. 29. (Frederick W. Pailthorpe is best known for providing 21 illustrations for the 1885 edition of Charles Dickens's *Great Expectations.*)

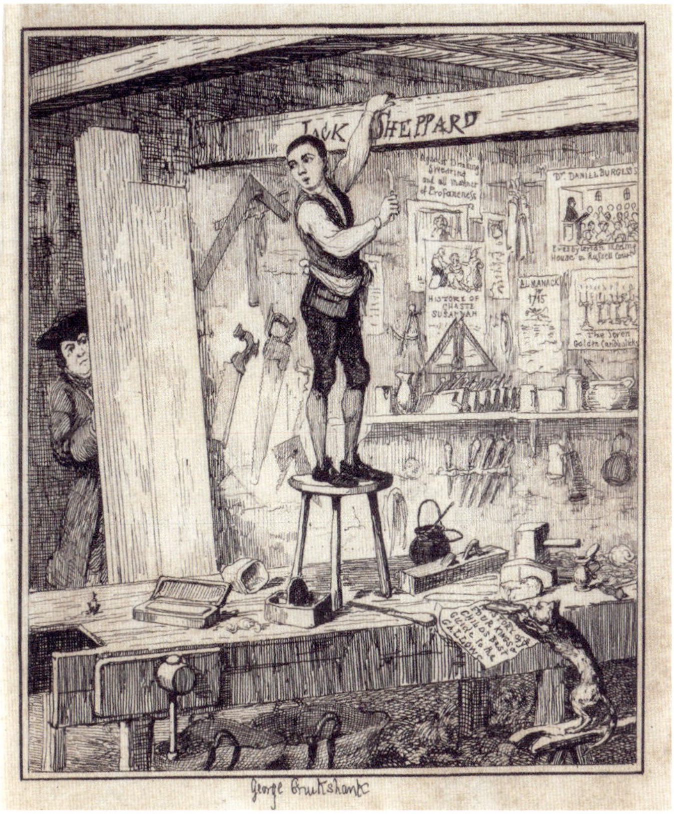

ITEM NO. 70.
Volume I: "The Name on the Beam," p. 152.

1841–1847: CRUIKSHANK'S DISPUTES WITH BENTLEY AND AINSWORTH; HIS REJECTION OF OFFERS FROM DICKENS AND PUNCH

70

Jack Sheppard. A Romance. By W. Harrison Ainsworth, Esq., Author of "Rookwood," and "Crichton." With Illustrations by George Cruikshank. In three Volumes. London: Richard Bentley, New Burlington Street. 1839.

71

Punch and the London Charivari, Volume the First. London: Published for the Proprietors, at the Office, 194, Strand, and Sold by All Booksellers. 1841. Containing the weekly issues of *Punch* from July through December 1841. Each issue had 12 pages, one of which contained a wood engraving entitled "Punch's Pencillings – No. I et seq."

PUNCH'S PENCILLINGS.—N°. XXII.

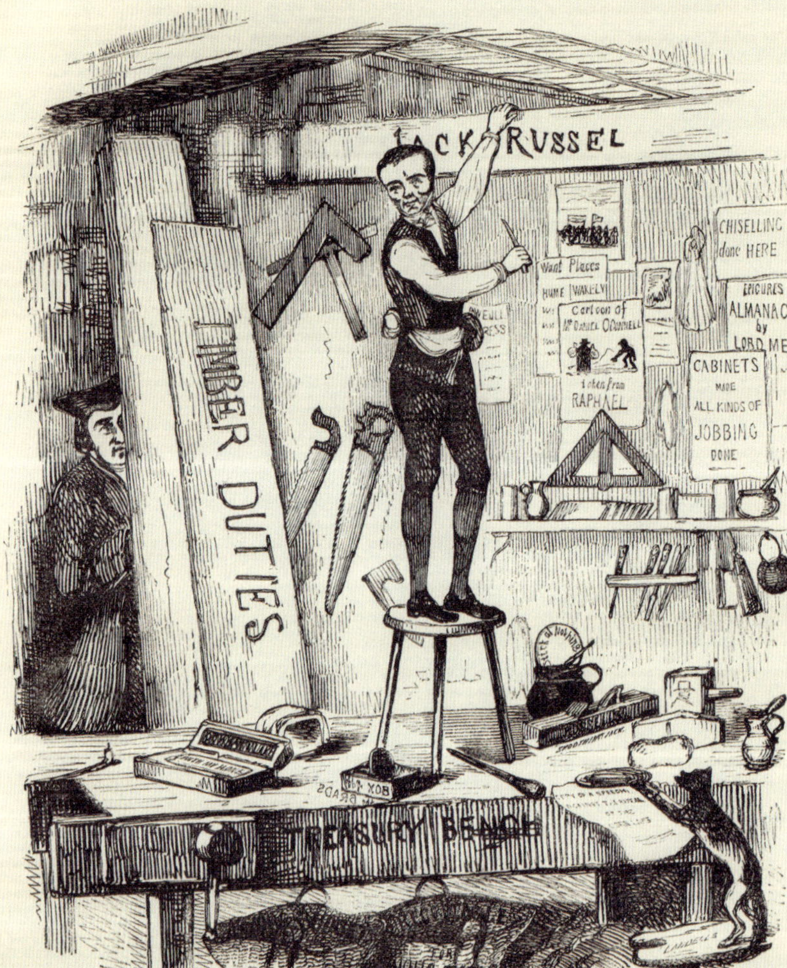

JACK CUTTING HIS NAME ON THE BEAM.

ITEM NO. 71. "Punch's Pencilling – No. XXII, Jack Cutting His Name On the Beam," December 11, 1841 issue, at p. 258, is a crudely executed rip-off by Ebenezer Landells of Cruikshank's illustration "The Name on the Beam" in *Jack Sheppard*. Perhaps this is one reason that Cruikshank refused to design for *Punch*. To see his work so poorly imitated surely added insult to injury.

72

Follies of the Year By John Leech, A Series of Coloured Etchings from Punch's Pocket Books – 1844–1864. With Some Notes by Shirley Brooks. Bradbury, Evans & Co., Bouverie Street, E.C. [1866].

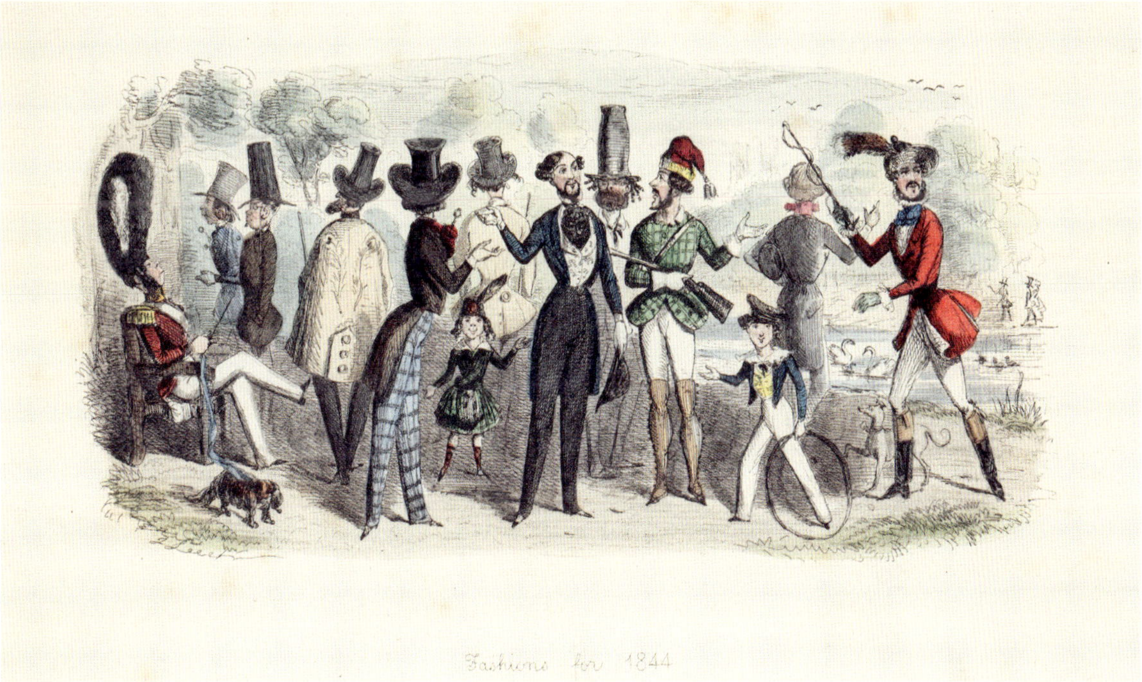

ITEM NO. 72. Plate: "Fashions of 1844."

73

George Cruikshank's Omnibus. Illustrated with One Hundred Engravings on Steel and Wood. Edited by Laman Blanchard, Esq. London: Tilt and Bogue, Fleet Street. MDCCCXLII.

74

The Bachelor's Own Book; or The Progress of Mr. Lambkin, (Gent.), in the Pursuit of Pleasure and Amusement, and also in Pursuit of Health and Happiness. In Twenty-Four Plates, designed and etched by George Cruikshank. Glasgow: David Bryce & Son, 129 Buchanan Street. [1883]. Third edition. This work was first published by Cruikshank and sold by David Bogue in 1844. The 24 etchings and original title page in this edition were all struck from the original steel plates and printed on 24 separate leaves.[90]

---

90. Cruikshank was surely influenced here by the recent works of the Swiss artist Rudolphe Topffer, whose *Histoire de M. Jabot* is said to have been the first comic book. Philipon's Aubert et Cie published the first French edition in Paris in 1839. An English adaptation entitled *The Adventures of Mr. Obadiah Oldbuck* was published by Tilt and Bogue in 1841.

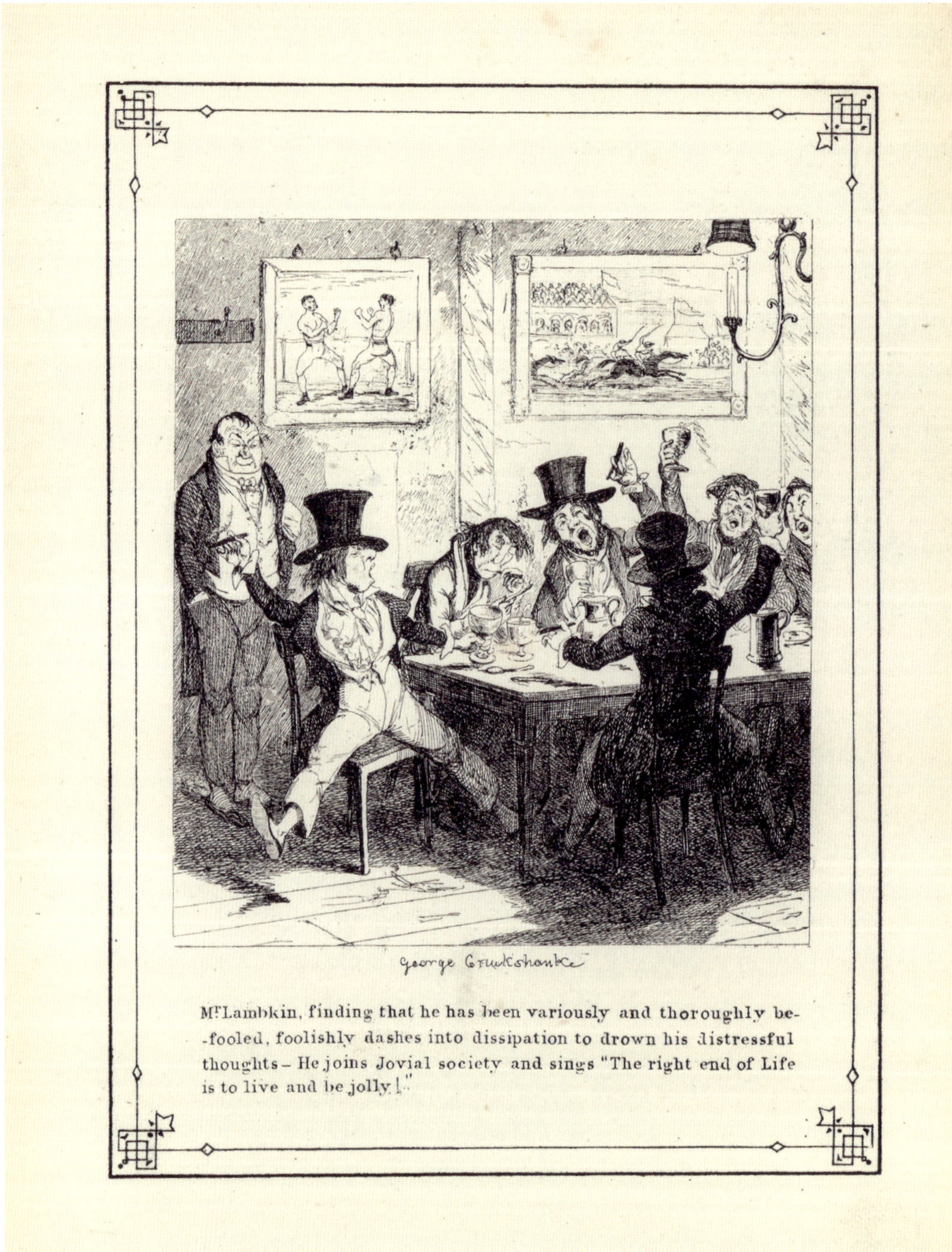

ITEM NO. 74. "Mr. Lambkin finding that he has been variously and thoroughly befooled, foolishly dashes into dissipation to drown his distressful thoughts – He joins Jovial society and sings 'The right end of Life is to live and be jolly!' "

75

George Cruikshank's Table Book. Edited by Gilbert Abbott à Beckett. Illustrated by George Cruikshank. In Twelve Monthly Parts. London: Published at the [Punch] Office, 194 Strand. 1845. Twelve steel etchings as the frontispieces to each of the parts, plus 116 woodcuts and glyphographs in text, all by Cruikshank. Contributors of text included Horace Mayhew, Mark Lemon, Gilbert à Beckett, and Michael Angelo Titmarsh [Thackeray]. Each part is in a buff wrapper designed by Cruikshank and engraved by W. J. Linton. All but one part (No. 6) has the same signature on top right corner of front wrapper, suggesting that this set (except No. 6) was retained by the original owner.

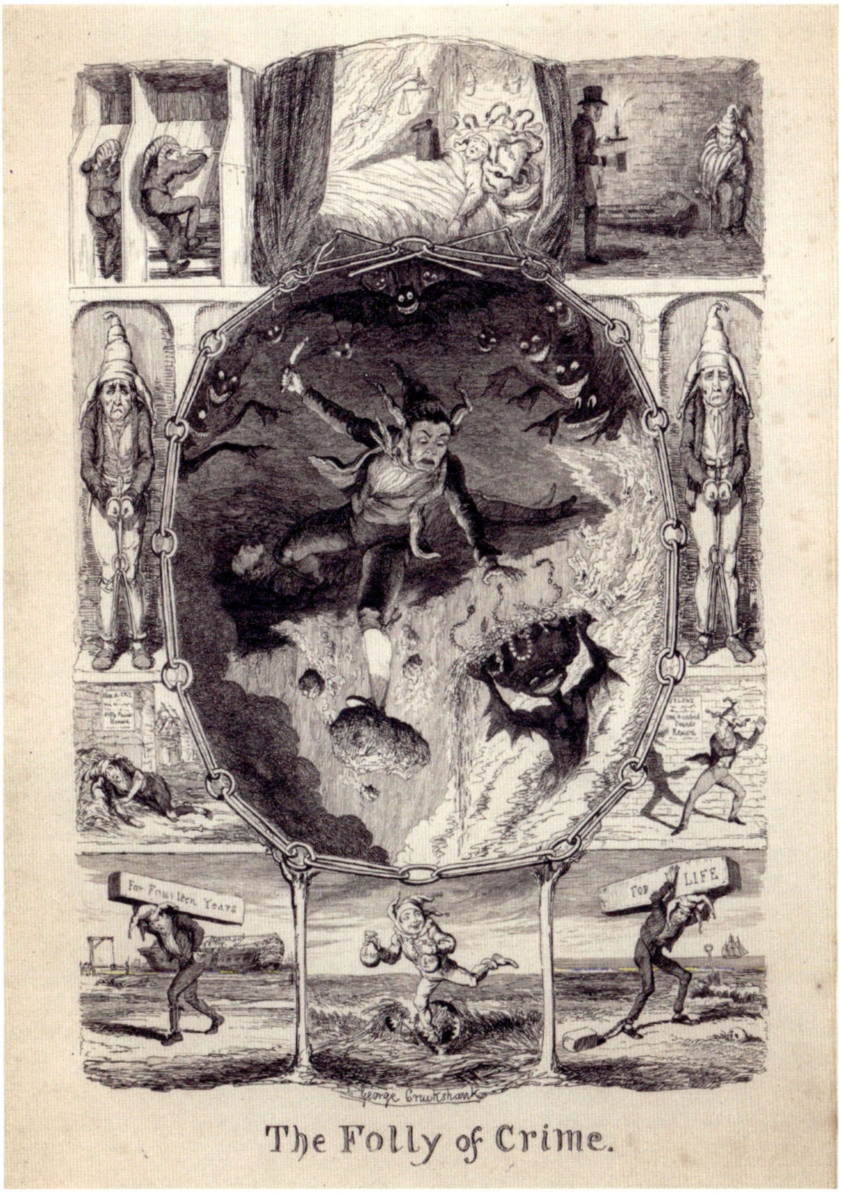

ITEM NO. 75. No. 3: Frontispiece: "The Folly of Crime."

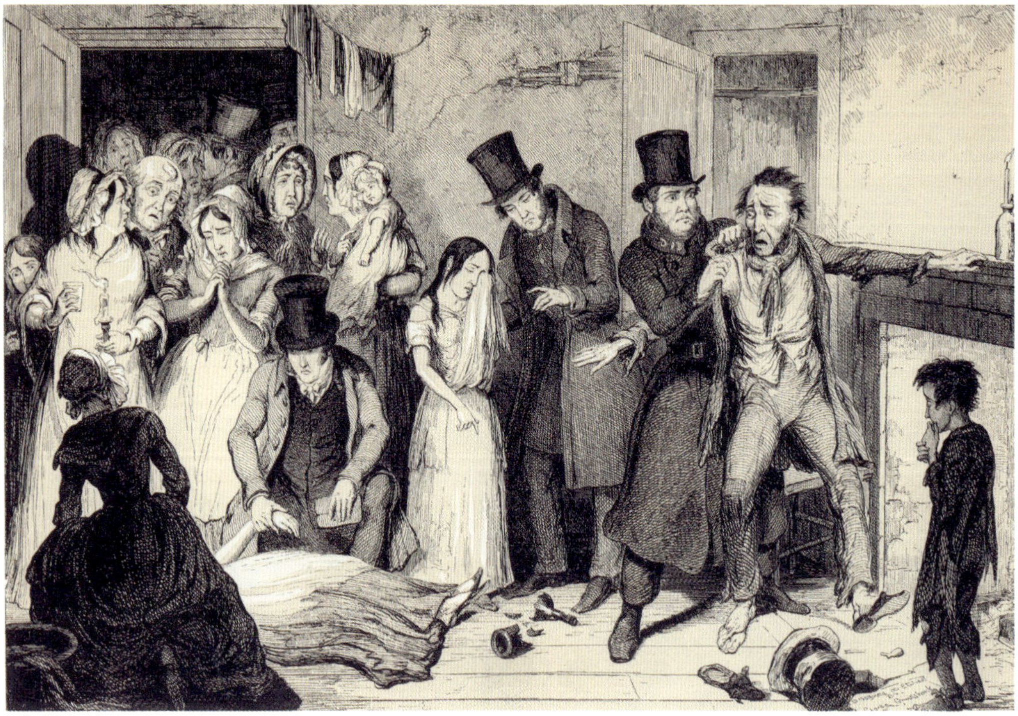

ITEM NO. 76A. Plate IV: "Fearful Quarrels, and Brutal Violence, are the Natural Consequences of the Frequent Use of the Bottle."

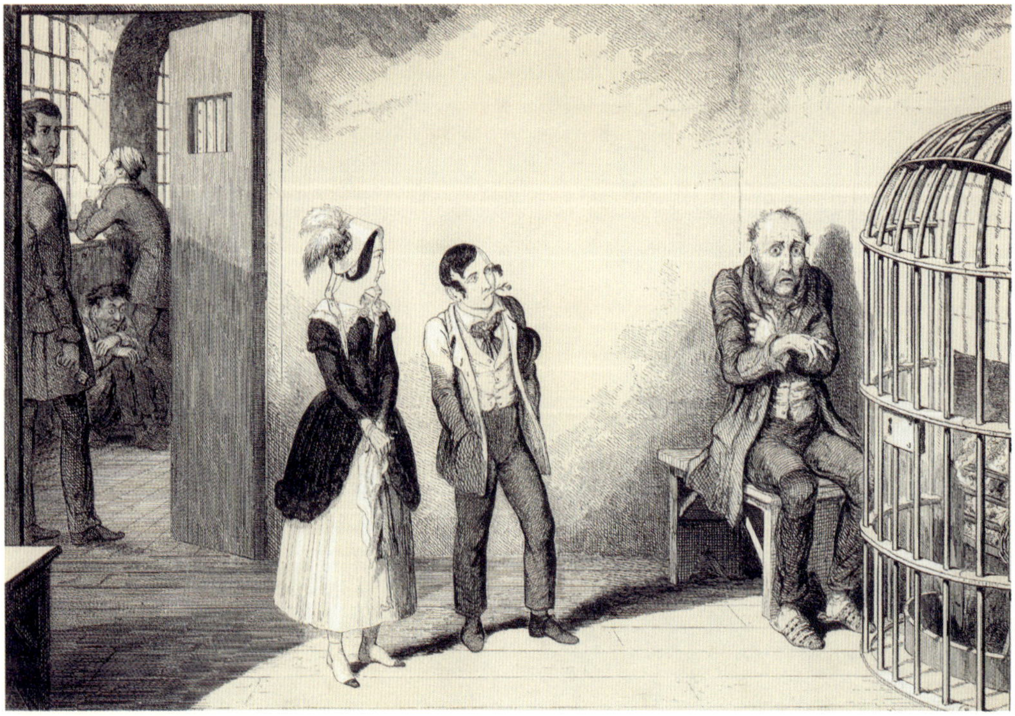

ITEM NO. 76B. Plate VIII: "The Bottle Has Done Its Work – It Has Destroyed the Infant and the Mother, It Has Brought the Son and Daughter to Vice and to the Streets, and Has Left the Father A Hopeless Maniac."

76

The Bottle, In Eight Plates Designed and Etched by George Cruikshank. Dedicated to Joseph Adshead, Esq. of Manchester. London: published for the author by David Bogue, 86 Fleet-Street. [1847]. Original publisher's binding, half-brown morocco over dark green linen-covered boards; title and facsimile of author's signature in gilt on top board. First edition of one shilling issue.

77

The Drunkard's Children, A Sequel to The Bottle. In Eight Plates by George Cruikshank. One Shilling. Published for the Artist, July 1st, 1848, By David Bogue, 86, Fleet Street, London; John Wiley and G.P. Putnam, New York; and J. Sands, Sydney, New South Wales, of whom may be had "The Bottle." An Edition of each Work is printed on Fine Paper in Imperial Folio with a Tint, Price Six Shillings. Publisher's original binding: red linen over boards with title in gilt on front cover with plain end papers. Title page pasted on recto of Plate I; Plates II–VIII are each printed on the recto of one leaf of heavy paper, eight leaves in all.

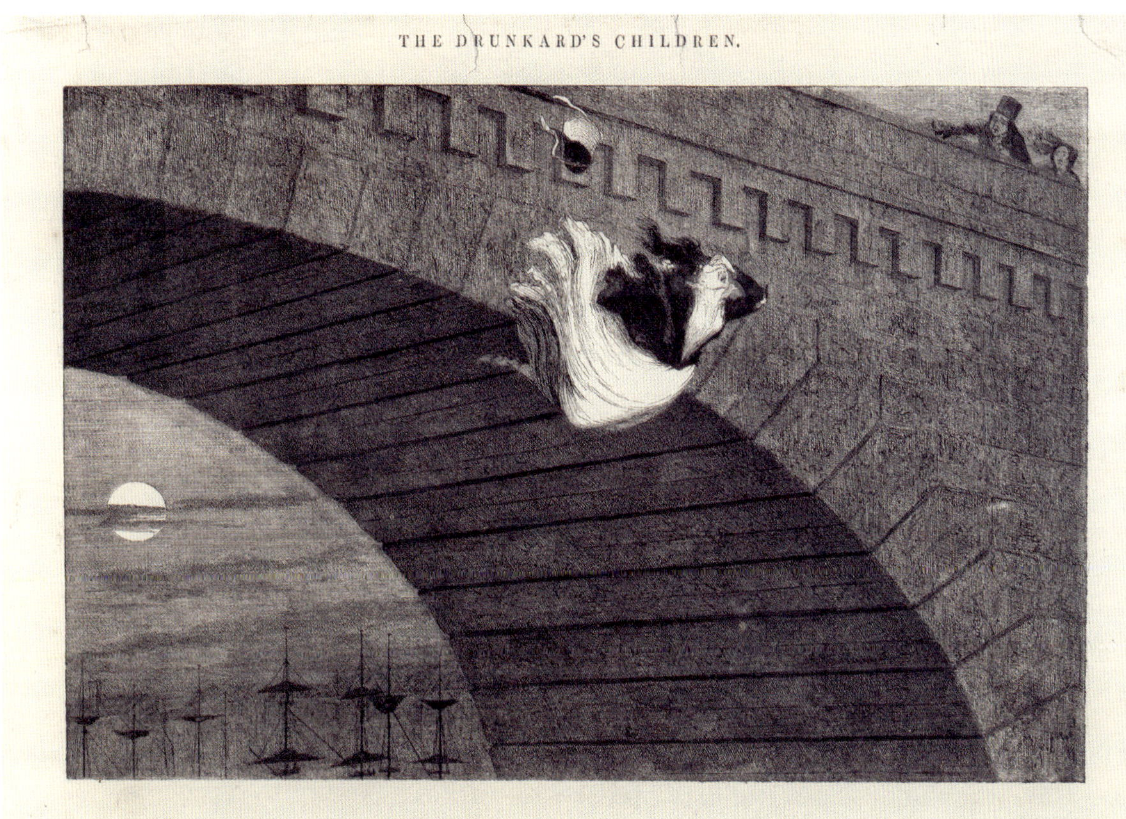

ITEM NO. 77. Plate VIII: "The Maniac Father and the Convict Brother are Gone – The Poor Girl, Homeless, Friendless, Deserted, Destitute, and Gin Mad, Commits Self Murder."

78

The Glass. The Bottle's Companion. n.a., n.p., n.d., no title page (title on spine). Binding by John Bumpus, 350 Oxford Street. A little mystery album. Eleven leaves with 21 hand-colored engraved scenes, each divided by a vertical black line cut into 11 pieces. The first, with only one scene, is pasted on the recto of the first linen leaf; the next two scenes are cut as one piece and pasted on the recto of the next leaf, and so on for nine more leaves with 18 more scenes. The British Art Center at Yale has the Abbey copy of this work, which they identify as having been published in 1850 in accordion fold format in the publisher's original brown cloth folder with title stamped in gilt on front cover. Publisher, author, and engraver are unknown. Clearly a parody of Cruikshank's *The Bottle.* Who was this witty artist/engraver? Perhaps Cruikshank himself? He loved to dash off these small, colorful little albums. The facial expressions are skilled and honed for amusement, and the hand-coloring is superb. On the other hand, the articulation of the figures does not appear to be quite up to our hero's talents. Most importantly, by then, surely Cruikshank had become much too serious about himself and his crusade for abstinence to make fun of his own work and the movement.

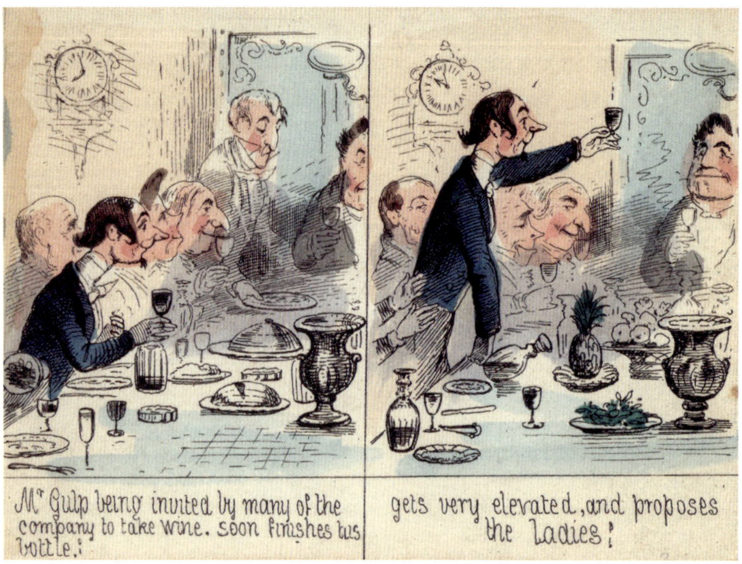

ITEM NO. 78. Scenes 2 & 3: "Mr. Gulp being invited by many of the company to take wine – soon finishes his bottle, gets very elevated, and proposes the ladies!"

79

The Good Genius that Turned Everything Into Gold or The Queen Bee and the Magic Dress, A Christmas Fairy Tale. By The Brothers Mayhew, with Illustrations by George Cruikshank. London. David Bogue, 86 Fleet Street. MDCCC XLVII. Original green and gilt wrappers and spine bound in rear. A perfect blend of fairy tale and Victorian morality tract, a precursor to *Cruikshank's Fairy Library.*

80

Whom to Marry and How To Get Married! Or, The Adventures of a Lady in Search of a Good Husband. Edited by The Brothers Mayhew. Illustrated by George Cruikshank. London: David Bogue, 86, Fleet Street. [1848]. First issued in six monthly parts from November 1847 to April 1848. Twelve etchings and a glyphographed title page.

81

1851: or The Adventures of Mr. and Mrs. Sandboys and Family Who Came Up to London to Enjoy Themselves and to See the Great Exhibition, by Henry Mayhew, and George Cruikshank. London: David Bogue, 86, Fleet Street. 1851. Eight foldout plates and a broadside with the speech of Prince Albert about the importance of the Great Exhibition, given at the Grand Banquet at the Mansion House on March 21st, 1850, pasted in rear.

82

The Palace of Glass; London in 1851. Designed by Watts Phillips and Percy Cruikshank. Drawn and Etched by Watts Phillips. Published by Ackermann & Co. 96 Strand. [1851]. Leporello. Much livelier than the scenes in the Mayhew/Cruikshank account, playing on Londoners' reaction to the hordes of foreigners arriving for the Great Exhibition.

83

No popery! A Protestant Roland for a Popish Oliver. By Anti Guy [pseud.] n.p. n.d. [George Augustus Sala] [London, R. Ackermann, 1850]. A small foldout book with 23 hand-colored woodcuts. Date is based on an orange broadside in the BMS, dated 1850, advertising this book with the following description: "Published as part of the furor against the restoration of the Roman Catholic hierarchy in England." Sala was a student of Cruikshank's and became a loyal friend in his later years.

84

Uncle Tom's Cabin. By Harriet Beecher Stowe. With Twenty-Seven Illustrations on Wood by George Cruikshank, Esq. London: John Cassell, Ludgate Hill. 1852. First Cruikshank illustrated edition, first issue. (The first English edition was published without illustrations a few weeks prior by C. H. Clarke.) WITH AUTOGRAPH LETTER FROM GCK TO PUBLISHER WITH QUESTIONS REGARDING HIS DRAWINGS PASTED IN.

85

George Cruikshank's Fairy Library. Published by D. Bogue, 86 Fleet St., Price One Shilling. Three volumes: *Hop-O'-My-Thumb* [1853], *Jack and the Bean Stalk* [1854], *Cinderella and the Glass Slipper* [1854]. A fourth volume, *Puss in Boots,* was published by Routledge, Warne, & Routledge, Broadway, Ludgate Hill. [1864]. Each in original wrapper with same pictorial etched design around a different medallion with title, on heavy blue paper. Six steel etchings in each volume. EXTRA-ILLUSTRATED with original drawings and watercolors for several of the etchings bound in.

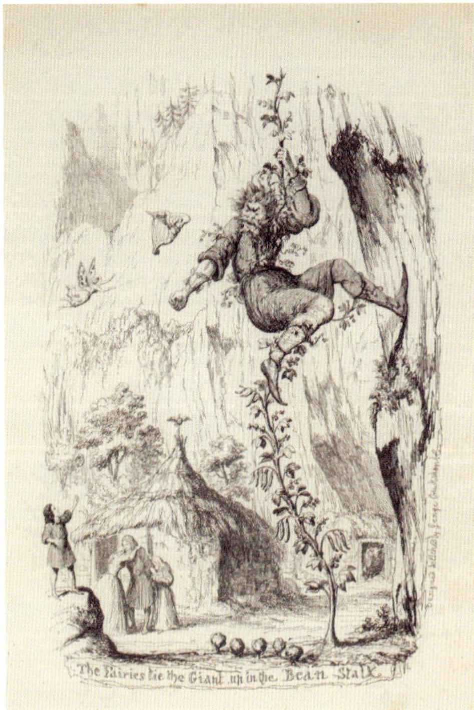

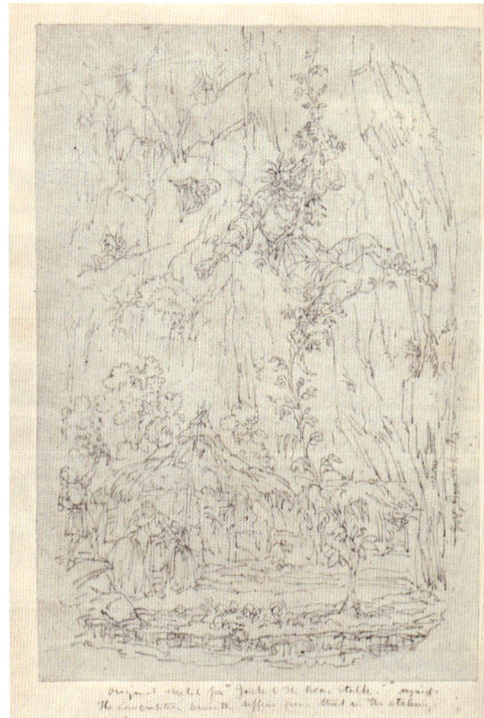

ITEM NOS. 85B & 85C. *Jack and the Bean Stalk*, "The Fairies tie the Giant, up in the Beanstalk," with original pencil drawing for etching bound in.*

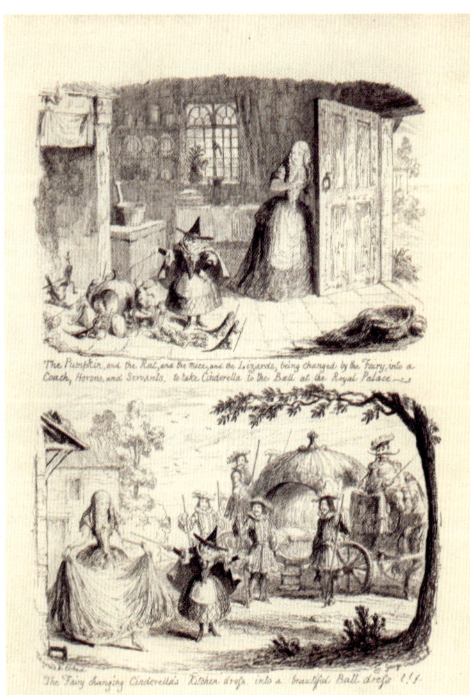

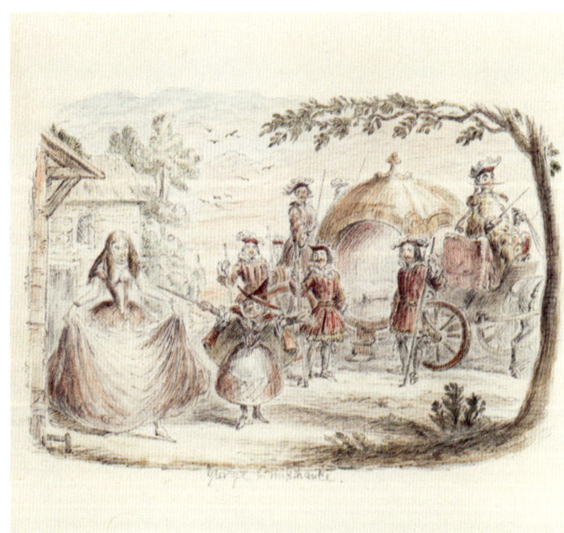

ITEM NOS. 85D & 85E. *Cinderella and the Glass Slipper*, "The Fairy Changing Cinderella's Kitchen Dress into a Beautiful Ball Dress!!" with original pencil and watercolor drawing bound in.

* For a comparison of an etching on steel with an etching on copper, compare Cruikshank's 1854 highly detailed and delicate etching of the giant trapped on the beanstalk, Item No. 85B, with the giant etched in 1826 for "The Young Giant and the Tailor," in Grimms' Tales, Item No. 38B.

ITEM NO. 85A. *Hop-O'-My-Thumb,* "The Giant Ogre discovers Hop-O'-My-Thumb & his brothers whom his wife had endeavored to conceal from him." See image on page 32.

86

A Letter from Hop-O'-My-Thumb to Charles Dickens, Esq. Upon "Frauds on the Fairies," "Whole Hog," &c., Published by D. Bogue, London [1854].

87

A Slice of Bread and Butter, cut by George Cruikshank. Being the substance of a speech delivered at a public meeting, held for the benefit of the Jews' and General Literary, and Mechanics' Institution. London, published by William Tweedie, 337, Strand. [1857]. With presentation note: "Rev. Hry Stebbing, D.D. With the best regards, yrs Geo Cruikshank." The Rev. Henry Stebbing officiated at the funeral of George's wife Mary Ann in 1849. This work tells of a pauper child who cannot be educated or given a place in society until he is imprisoned and sent to a reformatory school. It first appeared in 1857 and was reissued in the 1870s.

88

The Artist and the Author. A Statement of Facts by the Artist, George Cruikshank, Proving that the Distinguished Author, Mr. W. Harrison Ainsworth, is "laboring under a singular delusion" with respect to the origin of "The Miser's Daughter," "The Tower of London," etc. London: Bell and Daldy. [1872]. Written by Cruikshank after a spate of letters to the newspapers by Ainsworth and himself disputing the creative origination of Ainsworth's novels. The dispute was triggered by the staging in April 1872 of *The Miser's Daughter* adapted from Ainsworth's novel "but as usual relying primarily on [Cruikshank's] illustrations to create a succession of tableaux vivants." Sadly, notwithstanding the view of modern scholars demonstrating much of the truth of Cruikshank's claims of collaboration,[91] the Victorian critics were harsh on him, steeped as they were in the assumption that authors were the originators of the story, and that illustrators were hired to illustrate. George, now over 80 years old, made things worse by continuing to argue his case against both Ainsworth and Dickens in different venues and in strident terms.

89

Works of George Cruikshank Produced from 1799 to 1875. Consisting of upwards of Eleven Hundred Examples including Oil Paintings, Water Colour Drawings, and proof etchings. Printed for the Executive Committee for securing the Collection to the Nation. [1862]. [Title page

91. See, e.g., Patten, *George Cruikshank's Life,* 2:483–485; see also Wynn Jones, *George Cruikshank: His Life,* 13, 14. Jerrold labels Cruikshank's claims of collaboration a product of "his usual vehemence and wildness in statement, . . . utterly impossible for him to justify" (Jerrold, *Cruikshank in Two Epochs,* 1:252). However, as sole proof, he quotes a 12-page disquisition written by Ainsworth specifically for inclusion in Jerrold's biography after Cruikshank's death. Ibid., 1:258–269.

cut out.] This catalogue represents one of the stages in a 15-year saga encompassing the principal elements governing Cruikshank's life in its last two decades. In 1859, with his usual overestimation of his own powers, Cruikshank planned to create a massive oil painting, *The Worship of Bacchus*, in furtherance of the temperance movement, underwritten by numerous patrons, admirers, and fellow abstainers. The Testimonial Project, as it was known, went through several phases, exhibitions, and tours, including an exhibition in November 1862 in Exeter Hall, for which Cruikshank and his wife Eliza gathered eleven hundred of his other works to exhibit with *Bacchus* as an added attraction. A catalogue was produced for the exhibition. All efforts to secure a successful reception for the painting and the collected works failed, both critically and financially, and were followed by years of debt and dispute among the artist and his various underwriters. Even members of the Temperance League, to whom Cruikshank had looked for continued financial support, abandoned the project.

Finally, in late 1875, when he was in desperate need to rid himself of these crippling debts, his reputation once again made itself known. Two of his Royal Academy friends (thought to be the painters William Frith and Charles Landseer) came forward with an offer from the Royal Aquarium and Summer and Winter Garden Society to purchase the collection exhibited in Exeter Hall in 1862. The collection was again put on exhibition in order to help defray the costs of the sale; an "Executive Committee for securing the Collection to the Nation" (led by B. W. Richardson, Cruikshank's doctor and a trustee under his will) was created to help with fund-raising, and another catalogue was produced. The exhibition opened on August 1, 1876; the press was invited; Cruikshank's friend, William Stebbing, planted a favorable notice in *The Times*. But once again, no funds were cleared to help the Aquarium.[92] One of the most interesting aspects of this 15-year saga is the number of prestigious men from many backgrounds who were willing to invest in the "Immortal George" and his reputation.

90

Catalogue of a selection from the works of George Cruikshank, Esq., produced from 1799 to 1875, consisting of upwards of one hundred oil paintings, water-colour drawings, and original sketches, together with over a thousand proof etchings, &c., the property of the Royal Aquarium Society. Royal Aquarium, Westminster. This is the catalogue for the second exhibition, in 1876, described above.

91

Engraved Invitation to the Cruikshanks' Silver Wedding Anniversary, and a one-page printed notice entitled "Mr. & Mrs. George Cruikshank's Silver Wedding," dated at bottom "263 Hampstead Road, London, N.W., April, 1875," in which the Cruikshanks send effusive thanks to approximately 100 listed guests for attending their 25th wedding anniversary celebration on "Monday Afternoon, 8 of March, 1875." Among the attendees were Mrs. Charles Dickens

92. I have relied on Patten and on the information in the two catalogues listed above for this account. The facts provided by Patten are dispersed at various places in Volume 2, the final stages at pp. 489–492.

(Dickens had died in 1870) and the famous engravers, the brothers Dalziel (Edward and George). Of another 50 listed invitees "all of whom were unavoidably prevented from being present," only the gentry were singled out for particular note.[93] This copy of the notice is addressed in ink on the verso: "To Mr. and Mrs. William Stebbing" in Eliza Cruikshank's handwriting.

92

Six handwritten letters from George or Eliza Cruikshank to William Stebbing, Assistant Editor of *The Times,* dated variously from 1867 to 1875.

93

A Handbook for Posterity or Recollections of "Twiddle Twaddle." by George Cruikshank About Himself and Other People. A Series of Sixty-two "Etchings on Glass" with Descriptive Notes. London: W. T. Spencer, 27 New Oxford Street. 1896. Two hundred copies of this book were published after Cruikshank's death: 100 on India paper, 50 with colored etchings, and 50 in black and white. This copy is No. 19 of the 50 colored. The etchings were drawn on glass by Cruikshank and etched by Charles Hancock, the inventor of the glass etching process, who, in return for the etching blocks delivered to Cruikshank for one-half the price, received the ownership and copyright of the original drawings after Cruikshank's death. Ink inscription: "Geo Robertson, Esq. with every best wish, from W. T. Spencer, Jan 31st, 1900."

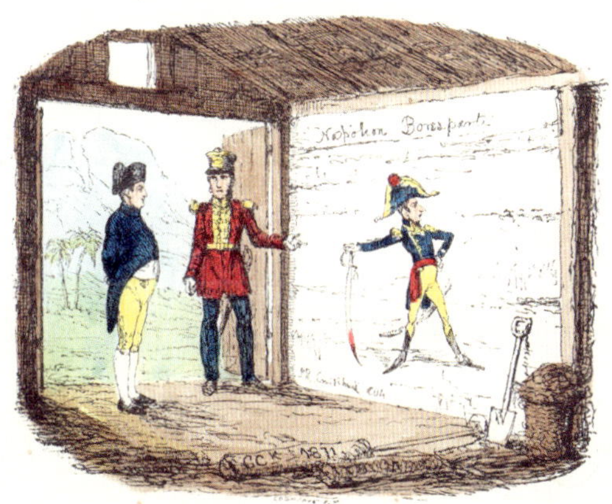
R. C. SHOWING NAPOLEON HIS SKETCH ON BARN WALL.

ITEM NO. 93B. No. 51. "Robert Showing Napoleon his Sketch on the Barn Wall [on St. Helena]."

ITEM NO. 93A. No. 6. "Outside the House in Dorset Square." Drawn by an elderly Cruikshank with handwritten notes indicating himself as a young daredevil holding on to the chimney (remember Sikes holding on to the chimney in *Oliver Twist*?), with his father's, then his own, studio on the top floor. See image on page 11.

---

93. One of the gentry, the Marquess of Lorne, is of personal interest to me. Two years after the Cruikshanks' silver wedding anniversary celebration, the young marquess, an artist and poet, was appointed Governor-General of Canada, and moved to Ottawa with his wife, the Princess Louise, fourth daughter of Queen Victoria. In 1880, he acquired land and fishing rights on the Grand Cascapedia River on the Gaspe Peninsula in Quebec, and built a house now known as Lorne Cottage. On his return to England in 1883, the marquess sold his land, Lorne Cottage, and all his fishing rights to my great-grandfather, Charles Barnes of Boston, and a partner. The camp and the river rights came down to my grandfather. I grew up hearing of my parents' trips north to Lorne Cottage, the 40- to 50-pound salmon killed on a particular rod with a particular fly, the guides, and the pools where the fishing was best, including one of the most treasured, the Princess Louise pool. See also Hoagy B. Carmichael, *The Grand Cascapedia River History* (North Salem, NY: Anesha Publishing, 2006), 1:24–42.

ACKNOWLEDGMENTS

I owe a great deal to a number of people for their help in assembling the works shown here and in producing this catalogue. My modest collection of Cruikshankiana comes from many sources. The most important have been my Grolier colleagues, Jim Cummins and his son, James, who always kept their eyes out for interesting pieces of the puzzle, and were the source of what is probably the gem of the collection: the album of proofs for *Sketches by Boz*, both series, assembled after Cruikshank's death by Henry Bruton, a major collector of Dickens and Cruikshank, with an interesting letter from Bruton to the album's next owner. Another of my Grolier friends in this endeavor has been Roy Young, who is responsible for much of my interesting material, including the large volume of Cruikshank's original drawings and watercolors collected by Adolf Zukor. I am also grateful to Benjamin Spademan, who was the source of much of my French collection and always comes up with unexpected treasures. Finally, I cannot leave out Swann Galleries, which I would haunt on a regular basis in the early days of my collecting and raise my paddle more often than I should have; or AbeBooks and eBay for their invaluable services. I must confess, whether browsing to see what is out there, or searching for that one item to fill a gap, I find online book shopping from my cozy kitchen to be addictive, fun and instructive . . . especially in a pandemic. In consequence, many of my books come from many different places scattered throughout the British, European, and U.S. countryside.

Turning to the catalogue, I am an amateur scholar whose primary source of contemporaneous information has been the prints, books, pamphlets, and bits and pieces in my collection. Thus, I have relied heavily on the scholarship of others in preparing the life and times of Mr. Cruikshank. Robert L. Patten's two-volume comprehensive, indeed encyclopedic, work, *George Cruikshank's Life, Times, and Art*, was my bible. I am heavily indebted to Mr. Patten for providing me with a well-lit path through the forest of Cruikshankiana. In fact, we have become pen pals recently as the result of my hunt for the original drawing of what is by far the most lively and amusing caricature of "the Great George" ever drawn, by the eminent British satirist Ronald Searle. It serves as the frontispiece for the 1974 collection of essays, *George Cruikshank: A Revaluation* edited by Mr. Patten, who became friends with Mr. Searle and is the proud owner of the drawing. We decided it was simply impractical to move it from Mr. Patten's wall in Houston to New York City.

With regard to identifying and describing the prints designed by Cruikshank, Gillray, and others in the early part of the century, I am indebted to the invaluable *Catalogue of Political and Personal Satires Preserved in the Department of Prints and Drawings in the British Museum* (1870–1954), edited from 1935 to 1954 by M. Dorothy George. And of course, Albert M. Cohn's 1924 *George Cruikshank, A Catalogue Raisonné* was essential. The other sources listed in the bibliography provided essential guideposts helping me to sort out and make sense of Cruikshank's multiple works and the arc of his long and complicated life.

As to the text, I am most appreciative of the review and wise comments of two dear comrades. Early on, my daughter, Josie Iselin, an accomplished author and marine scholar, was good enough to read my manuscript and give me very useful and insightful comments. Later, as I got further into my research, I asked my friend Cynthia Roman, Curator of Prints, Drawings, & Paintings at the Lewis Walpole Library at Yale University, if she would review what I had done. She kindly agreed, and as a result, my world expanded and my research became far richer. Lastly, I want to thank Chris Loker, the stalwart Chair of the Publications Committee of the Grolier Club, for her encouragement and guidance.

I am very indebted to my copy editor, Janice Fisher, for her highly skilled ability to put my copy into final form. She has been most patient in dealing with the challenges presented by so many numbered pieces of the puzzle that had to be presented in readable fashion. Many thanks also to Bob Lorenzson and his wife Dominique, who took the beautiful photographs of the plates and illustrations. Lastly, I am most grateful to the impresario of catalogue designers, Grolier colleague Jerry Kelly. The pictures tell the story, but the story of a comic artist must have vitality, which Jerry's design has achieved with aplomb.

Lastly, once again, I want to thank my five children, their spouses, and my 14 grandchildren for the quiet support they have given me over the years for my bibliographic obsession. They have watched my collecting habits sprout from a few tentative forays into a rather consuming and expensive passion, expressing only generous encouragement and pleasure.

BIBLIOGRAPHY

Bates, William, B.A., M.R.C.S.E., Etc. *George Cruikshank: The Artist, The Humourist, and The Man, With Some Account of His Brother Robert. A Critico-Bibliographical Essay.* Birmingham: Houghton and Hammond, Scotland Passage, 1878.

British Museum, and M. Dorothy George. *Catalogue of Political and Personal Satires Preserved in the Department of Prints and Drawings in the British Museum.* London: British Museum Publications, 1935–1954.

Carmichael, Hoagy B. *The Grand Cascapedia River History.* 2 vols. North Salem, NY: Anesha Publishing, 2006.

Cohn, Albert M. *George Cruikshank, A Catalogue Raisonné of the Work Executed During the Years 1806-1877, With Collations, Notes, Approximate Values, Facsimiles, and Illustrations.* London: The Bookman's Journal, 1924.

Cruikshank, George, William Harrison Ainsworth, William Maxwell, and Charles Dickens. *Cruikshank's Water-Colours, with Introduction by Joseph Grego.* London: A. & C. Black, 1903.

Dalziel, George, and Edward Dalziel. *The Brothers Dalziel, A Record of Fifty Years' Work in Conjunction with Many of the Most Distinguished Artists of the Period 1840–1890.* London: Methuen and Co., 1902.

Eckel, John C. *The First Editions of the Writings of Charles Dickens and Their Values, A Bibliography.* London: Chapman & Hall, Ltd., 1913.

Gatrell, Vic. *City of Laughter: Sex and Satire in Eighteenth-Century London.* New York: Walker & Company, 2006.

George, M. Dorothy. *Hogarth to Cruikshank: Social Change in Graphic Satire.* New York: Walker & Company, 1967.

Hardie, Martin. *English Colored Books.* New York: G. P. Putnam's Sons; London: Methuen and Co., 1906.

Haywood, Ian. *The Rise of Victorian Caricature.* Cham, Switzerland: Palgrave Macmillan, an imprint of Springer Nature Switzerland AG, [2020].

Jerrold, Blanchard. *The Life of George Cruikshank in Two Epochs.* 2 vols. London: Chatto and Windus, 1882.

Maidment, Brian. "Graphic Satire, Caricature, Comic Illustration and the Radical Press, 1820–1845." In *Journalism and the Periodical Press in Nineteenth-Century Britain,* edited by Joanne Shattuck, 84–103. Cambridge: Cambridge University Press, 2017. doi:10.1017/9781316084403.007.

Maidment, Brian. "The Draughtsman's Contacts: Robert Seymour and the Humorous Periodical Press in the 1830s." *Journal of European Periodical Studies* 1, no. 1 (Summer 2016).

Maidment, Brian. "'Larks in Season': *The Comic Almanack* (1835–54)." *Cahiers victoriens et édouardiens* [Enligne], 84 Automne, 2016, mis enligne le 01 novembre 2016, consulté le 22 avril 2017, http://cve.revues.org/2881, doi:10.4000/cve.2881.

Patten, Robert L. *George Cruikshank's Life, Times and Art.* Vol. 1: 1792–1835; Vol. 2: 1835–1878. New Brunswick, NJ: Rutgers University Press, 1992.

Patten, Robert L., ed. *George Cruikshank: A Revaluation. The Princeton University Library Chronicle* 35, nos. 1 and 2 (Autumn, Winter 1973–74).

Ray, Gordon N. *The Illustrator and the Book in England from 1790 to 1914.* New York: The Pierpont Morgan Library, Oxford University Press, 1976.

Spielmann, M. H. *The History of "Punch."* New York: The Cassell Publishing Co., 31, East 17th Street (Union Square), 1895.

Thackeray, William Makepeace. "An Essay on the Genius of George Cruikshank," *The Westminster Review* 34, no. 1 [1840].

Tooley, R. V. *English Books with Coloured Plates, 1790–1860, A Bibliographical Account of the Most Important Books Illustrated by English Artists in Colour Aquatint and Colour Lithography* (2d ed.). London: B. T. Batsford Ltd., 1954.

Wynn Jones, Michael. *George Cruikshank: His Life and London.* London: Macmillan London Limited, 1978.

Set in the types of William Caslon III.
Design & typography by
Jerry Kelly.